Dear

planes!

Lots of love

26/3

£4-25

RETURN TO RHINEBECK

It was great to see this immaculate 230 hp Wright-powered Pitcairn PA-7 Mailwing arrive for the Golden Biplane fly-in at Old Rhinebeck. It was an even greater pleasure to meet the pilot and owner Mr Stephen Pitcairn, whose father Mr Harold F. Pitcairn had designed and built these beautiful mail and sport planes. Dating from 1927, about 150 of them were built. Stephen, who is obviously very proud of his family's aviation history, owns four more airworthy Mailwings, one PA-5, one PA-6, another PA-7 and one PA-8, as well as a PCA-2 Autogyro. Another of his family's Pitcairn Autogyros has been presented to the EAA Museum at Oshkosh.

RIGHT:
The sun has risen on a beautiful summer's day at Old Rhinebeck. The show aircraft are being brought out for a clean-up and check before most of the spectators arrive. The Curtiss JN-4H Jenny ground crew wait for the Sopwith Camel to be pushed out to the flight line to join two Great Lakes trainers and a Howard DGA-15P.

RETURN TO RHINEBECK

Flying
Vintage
Aeroplanes

Mike Vines

Airlife

England

ACKNOWLEDGEMENTS

USA

I realise how important it is to talk to as many people as possible when researching a book, even if it is for only a couple of minutes each. For in that time, as happened many times at Old Rhinebeck, you can gain a whole new insight into a subject, or pick up further clues, and produce a book which will hopefully do justice to its subject. I must therefore give thanks to quite a considerable number without whose contributions this book would have been much poorer.

Thank you to Rita Palen, a wonderful and private lady who put up with my questioning amidst a very busy Sunday show. Thanks to Kay Bainbridge who gave me an incredible insight into her life with husband Gordon and their great friendship with Cole Palen, which was invaluable for the chapter 'The Early Years'. To Jim Hare, for his time, hospitality and patience, and especially for checking the manuscript of this book. Thanks also to Gene DeMarco for showing me the location of Old Rhinebeck's treasure trove which is not on public view, and for flying me on several quickly arranged air-to-air sorties in his Stampe SV.4b. To Ken Cassens, thank you for your help in letting us spend time in your office and filing cabinets checking out the histories of Old Rhinebeck's aircraft collection. A special thank you to pilot Bill King who flew me

in his Tiger Moth on countless sorties. To Brian Coughlin, many thanks for staying airborne for so long in your beautiful Fokker D.VIII so that I could photograph you properly. To Ed Hammerle for the flights in a Cub and his Great Lakes. Thanks to Stanley Segalla for his great stories that helped me visualize Cole Palen in the early years and for a masterclass display of crazy flying. Thanks to those old friends re-met, John Barker and Karl Erickson, and to a new friend who has really got the pioneer aircraft bug – Dan Taylor. A thank you to Dick King for his great Cole Palen stories and for his accurate flying of the Curtiss Jenny and Great Lakes for me on air-to-air photo sorties. His wonderful book *The Skies Over Rhinebeck* (by Richard King with Stephen Wilkinson, published by Jostens in the USA in 1997) was a great source of material for the 'The Early Years' chapter and is a great read. Last, but certainly not least, my thanks to volunteer Hugo Visconti who took me under his wing like an elder brother and who taught me an awful lot about the aircraft and the great people that still congregate at Cole Palen's aerodrome.

ENGLAND

Thanks to Birmingham International Airport's managing director Brian Summers for his help in getting us from Birmingham to New York, via British Airways, so quickly and smoothly. Leaving Birmingham mid-morning (UK time) we arrived at Rhinebeck, 100 miles north of JFK, at six p.m. local time.

Thanks to Simon Morris of Dunn's Imaging plc for his clean E-6 transparency processing of my seventy rolls of film. Thanks also to Mike Dolling of Kodak Ltd for his advice and his company's wonderfully warm Kodak 100SW film which was exclusively used for this book on 35mm and 120 roll film. Thanks also to Roger Brindley of KJP Ltd, Birmingham for his help in lens selection for my Nikon F.4, F.5 and Mamiya 6×4.5 cameras.

Last but not least, on this side of the ocean my thanks go to my wife Frances who researched through filing cabinets and dug around in dusty hangars while I was photographing the treasures of Old Rhinebeck. She also helped turn the stack of scribblings we arrived home with into the following book.

Mike Vines
Birmingham, England

Copyright © 1998 Mike Vines

First published in the UK in 1998
by Airlife Publishing Ltd

British Library Cataloguing-in-Publication Data
A catalogue record for this book is available from the British Library

ISBN 1 85310 975 4

Typeset by Servis Filmsetting Ltd, Manchester, England.
Printed in Singapore

Airlife Publishing Ltd
101 Longden Road, Shrewsbury, SY3 9EB, England

CONTENTS

The very essence of Old Rhinebeck is and always has been the friendliness and warmth of the cast to the audience. It probably goes back to the very early days when Cole Palen and his pals were totally surprised that anyone should take any interest in what they were doing. Here Brian Coughlin, who is the Black Baron today, explains the intricacies of his Fokker D.VIII repro to fascinated visitors.

INTRODUCTION

It might sound corny but in the beginning there was just Cole Palen, a twenty-five-year-old all-American boy from New York State, who by a twist of fate came face-to-face with six World War One aeroplanes on which he spent his life savings. This decision was to take him over, change his life and inspire and influence hundreds of thousands of like-minded people throughout the world.

In this book, through interviews with Cole's surviving loyal band of friends and relatives and from tapes recorded with Cole in 1990, I hope to shine some new light on the man who was a legend in his own lifetime. And show that his dream of keeping these fragile and temperamental aeroplanes flying lives on after his sudden death in December 1993.

Thanks to Cole and Rita Palen's foresight the collection at Old Rhinebeck has become a non-profit-making educational corporation. This one unselfish act has saved the aerodrome and kept its aeroplanes, vehicles and artifacts in safe-keeping for the American nation and thereby for the rest of the world. It is still a living museum and every weekend, mid-June to mid-October, new generations get to smell burnt castor oil, hear and see old rotary aero-engines in the air and have a chance to relive the pioneering days of aviation from the earliest flying machines through World War One up to the Lindbergh era.

Over the years at Old Rhinebeck an incredible amount of knowledge has been amassed and passed onto the next generations so that the skills involved in rebuilding and rerigging these early flying machines are not lost. If these early aeroplanes and their working engines had not been preserved, then this knowledge would probably have been lost for ever as most of the early aircraft designers were notorious for not keeping proper records. Thankfully Cole Palen saw the need for this preservation of knowledge, which will continue under the educational corporations he set up, and be available to anyone who wants to know.

The Saturday shows at Old Rhinebeck feature their pioneer aircraft dating from 1909 to 1914. You can see the oldest original aeroplane flying in the United States, a fragile original Blériot XI, rise gently into the air if the wind is calm enough; it has reached an incredible height of sixty feet on occasions. But even on a perfect day, so delicate are these pioneer aircraft that, they are only flown in a straight line on Rhinebeck's switchback runway and never above the tree line in case a sudden gust of wind should render them uncontrollable. Spectators are invited to question the pilots about these early airplanes; you can learn how the wing warping works, or how fast they fly. It's an amazing chance to learn at first hand what it's like to fly these antique airplanes.

But what makes Old Rhinebeck different from all the other flying museums is the Cole Palen philosophy that 'learning can be fun'. To watch the cast of the Sunday shows re-enacting the eternal triangle of The Black Baron, Trudy Truelove and Sir Percy Goodfellow to the backdrop of World War One dogfights and bombing raids, is to see that the cast are enjoying performing the loony melodrama just as much as the crowd is enjoying watching them. You can be absolutely sure that on every Sunday show day, on the dot of four p.m., the dastardly Black Baron will meet his horrible end. But as surely as the sun rises every morning he'll be back, just as evil and just as scheming, flying his Fokker Triplane.

Cole's dream is still alive! Let's celebrate it!

Old Rhinebeck Aerodrome is situated in the beautiful Hudson Valley (a two-hour drive from Manhattan). About three miles north of the town of Rhinebeck on Route 9 make a right turn at the Aerodrome Sign and drive about another mile until you see the entrance.

Weather permitting the airshows take place every Saturday and Sunday from mid-June through to mid-October. The fashion show starts at two p.m. and the flying starts at two-thirty prompt.

For further information contact:

Rhinebeck Aerodrome Museum
44 Stone Church Road
Rhinebeck
NY 12572
USA

Telephone: (914) 758 8610
Facsimile: (914) 758 6481
Website: // www Old Rhinebeck.org

An original Avro 504K was one of the six aircraft that Cole bought in 1951 from the Roosevelt Museum. This famous World War One British training aircraft was built in 1966 under the supervision of Vivian Bellamy, for a movie which was never made. It is, however, powered by a 110 hp Le Rhône rotary engine from the correct period and like the original aircraft does not have any brakes.

THE EARLY YEARS

When people find out I've visited Old Rhinebeck they bombard me with questions. Did you ever get to meet Cole Palen? What was he like? How did he get started? For all these and probably thousands more out there who want to know the answers, this chapter is for you.

I interviewed Cole in 1990 when he was sixty-five, and have since spoken to his widow Rita, and many colleagues and friends such as Stanley Segalla, Dick and Bill King, Kay Bainbridge and Jim Hare, plus many others who have been part of the Old Rhinebeck scene for so many years.

Cole was born James H. Palen on 29 December 1925 in Pennsylvania, but soon after his parents moved house to a small chicken farm near Poughkeepsie, New York, right next to the airport. 'I grew up at that airport and boy was it exciting! The airport opened around 1929 and closed in thirty-six or thirty-seven; a short time, but it was the period when Lindbergh had flown across the ocean and aviation was the up and coming thing. Poughkeepsie had an airport and that's where I got the bug,' explained Cole.

He'd got the bug all right, for at five years old he came across an aircraft starting crank embedded in his folks' backyard. To Cole it had obviously fallen out of an aeroplane. He returned it to its grateful owner, the legendary barnstormer John Miller, who lived close by; sure enough it was his crank which had fallen out of his biplane during aerobatics practice a year earlier. Cole got his first aeroplane ride when he was ten years old in a Standard J-1.

When Cole finished high school he was drafted into the US Army in August 1944 as an infantryman during the Battle of the Bulge. He witnessed the Allied 'thousand bomber raids' over Europe from the trenches. In 1946 he was back home and under the GI Bill he entered the Roosevelt Aviation School, at Roosevelt Field, Long Island, to train as a mechanic. After graduating with a mechanic's license he got himself a 'conventional' job, learnt to fly for $62.50, soloed after eight hours, and bought himself a 40hp Piper Cub. 'I flew the Cub for about 170 hours in a few months, crashed it and it burnt up while I was fixing it – I was out of aviation for four years from 1947 to 1951,' he commented sadly. The 'giant leap back', as he termed it, was when he bought part of the Roosevelt Field Museum collection in 1951:

I knew about Hangar 68 from 1947 when I got my AP license at Roosevelt Field. Nine ex-museum aircraft were piled up on one side in a dirty, dusty and disassembled condition, but I used to sit in the cockpits – boy I thought it was great. I even went along to see the president of Roosevelt Field; I was just a kid with no money but I asked him the status of the aeroplanes [raucous laughter]. In 1951, when I heard that Roosevelt Field was to become a shopping mall I stole into Hangar 68 – the nine planes were still there. Three of them were going to the Smithsonian, but Mr Guthrie, Roosevelt Field president, told me to make an offer for the others. I offered my life savings as a private in the infantry; I had never wanted anything so much before. In case I couldn't afford them all I made a separate offer for the Sopwith Snipe. I wanted it more than all the other five aircraft put together.

Cole's offer for all six was accepted and at the age of twenty-five he became the proud owner of a Sopwith Snipe, a SPAD XIII, a Curtiss Jenny, an Avro 504K, an Aeromarine 39B and a Standard J-1. How much did he pay for these classic veterans? Well, Cole was a little shy of answering this particular question, but his friends reckoned he paid $1,500 for the lot.

The next problem he faced was how to get them all from Roosevelt Field to his father's farm inside a thirty-day time limit:

I chose to move the Curtiss Jenny first because surprisingly the tires were 'up'. I couldn't understand this after all those years but never the less I stuck the tail of the fuselage into the trunk of my 1948 Hillman Minx convertible and started off. A little while later, bowling along at thirty mph, I noticed that there were pieces of something flying out of the Jenny's wheels. Guess what, they'd made nice wooden shims inside the tires to make it look like they were 'up'. It shows how naive I was. We tried all sorts of things including tying rags and bits of inner tube around the wooden wheels, but with an almighty twang the spokes of one wheel finally gave out in the trolley tracks. There was a trolley right behind me but fortunately I managed to pull over onto an empty lot, and after repairing the wheel I finally struggled home.

Eventually, after exhausting most of his friends and relatives – they would only do one trip each – all six aircraft were safely home. 'This was a low-budget operation,' said Cole. 'The planes were positioned nose-down tail-up in a quarter of my father's barn which I rented.'

He then set about getting them into flying condition –

starting with the SPAD XIII. 'I first cut a small hole in the fabric of the wing, stuck my nose in and had a good sniff – no mice, it smelt great.' The radiator, cowling, exhaust pipes and prop were missing, but undaunted Cole set to getting the 235 hp water-cooled V-8 engine back in running order. Overcoming 'minor snags', as he modestly called them, the SPAD was eventually transported to Stormville Airport for its first flight. This was the first time Cole had flown an open-cockpit biplane – a huge jump from Piper Cubs and Aeroncas. His first flight was a twenty-foot-high hop, but by the fourth flight he was up to 3,000 feet. However, on landing he ground-looped and finished up ten feet from the hangar doors – which were closed at the time. Reasoning that if he was going to write it off he might as well fly it some more, on the next trip he flew for over thirty minutes. 'It climbed great, it flew great and it scared me to death, but I flew it for the fun of it and didn't ground-loop too often. A friend also flew it and he ground-looped too!'

Around 1956 he met Frank Tallman (this was before the Tallmantz Corporation was set up). 'A great guy, a showman and a great pilot,' remarked Cole. He suggested sending the SPAD and a Blériot which Cole had acquired to Hollywood to appear in a movie. This was to be a turning point in Cole's life. 'It turned out to be a lousy picture but the money was good and I really needed the money. All this time my parents must have wondered where I was heading, but they were just wonderful and let me get on with flying and restoration projects.'

'Chocks away!' Ken Cassens is raring to go fly in the Avro 504K; Gene DeMarco, far side, and Dan Taylor (in appropriate white A.V. Roe overalls) clear the offending 'blocks'.

LEFT:
Young Sean Grim is dwarfed by the Avro 504K. He was seen earlier helping his dad fix the engine of a Maxwell 1910 auto, until he saw that the ground crew needed a hand in moving the Avro. He thinks it's great wearing period clothes for the Rhinebeck shows and when asked what he wanted to be when he was grown up, as quick as a flash he said, 'A pilot!' Exactly the same answer Cole gave to his grandma at the same age.

BELOW:
The Avro 504K was acquired by Cole in 1971 and has been extensively flown in the 'bomber raids' at Old Rhinebeck ever since. This machine copies the yellow and black checkerboard period color scheme as produced by Morgan & Co. Ltd of Leighton Buzzard, England. The 504 started life as a light bomber, and three British machines successfully bombed the Zeppelin Airship sheds at Friedrichshafen in 1914. Armed only with four 20 lb bombs each, they managed to score a direct hit and blew up a fully inflated Zeppelin.

With the money earned from his movie work he was able to start looking around for a property. 'I didn't think of a museum, just a little field, a tie-down so that my father could have his barn back.' He bought a derelict farm at Rhinebeck in November 1958. 'The fact that the previous owner had been murdered in the house helped keep the price down,' laughed Cole. With the help of friends and a lot of struggle a runway was slowly hacked out of the forest.

Now with somewhere to live right alongside his own airfield, Cole set about collecting and restoring more aeroplanes. Over the years he bought, sold, swopped and loaned aircraft and eventually only two of the original six remained – the SPAD and the Snipe. The Snipe, powered by a 130 hp Clerget, first flew from Old Rhinebeck in 1962 and was a regular performer until 1966 when it suffered an engine failure. It was rebuilt by Cole's closest collaborator Gordon Bainbridge, but wasn't flown again and was bequeathed to the National Air and Space Museum Washington DC in Cole's Will.

Slowly word spread about these beautiful aeroplanes and people turned up to see them. Cole was surprised that people were interested but demand increased and more and more people kept coming, so engines were run and aeroplanes flown. 'By 1966 we had a "hat at the gate", it was all nickels and dimes and didn't really pay for anything – but that's how Old Rhinebeck started.'

Cole had lived alone with just parts of his aeroplanes to keep him company until he married Rita Weidner at the age of forty-two. Rita took over the administrative side of Cole's affairs and slowly bank statements started to appear in the black which, according to friends, was a distinct rarity. Rita and her sister Marion still run the shop at Old Rhinebeck on weekends. 'I first met Cole at a New Year's Eve party in 1964 on the coldest day I can ever remember. I didn't find out immediately what was driving him but I did find out that he was a genuine person and that didn't take long,' Rita told me. When she did find out, she wasn't sure if she could handle it at first, which was not surprising. For when she moved into the house there was still a brick's width gap under one window where the sill had been removed (in fact the whole window frame plus the sill had been taken out at one time to get one of Cole's aeroplanes out). 'I improved the kitchen, but the doors wouldn't lock and he was finishing off the Fokker Triplane in the living room,' she remembers.

Long-time Rhinebeck stalwart Dick King has been flying from Old Rhinebeck Aerodrome for thirty-seven of its thirty-eight years.

In the early days it was just a dirt runway of just over a thousand feet long bordered by dismayingly tall trees. Spectators wandered in by accident and usually were outnumbered by the volunteers – some of whom drove four-hour round trips just to put on their uniforms and help stage this extravaganza. But Cole was rapidly accumulating one of the finest private collections in the world, and with more and more aircraft to work with the scripts for the shows became more of a melodrama – live theater for airplane enthusiasts. For the people who

made it all come into being it has truly been a labor of love. People like Gordon Bainbridge, Bob Love, Dave Fox, Bob Tator, Tom Stark, Stanley Segalla and many more volunteered for many hours of pushing, hammering, painting, rock picking, mowing, tinkering, welding, flying, announcing – whatever it took to put on the show. None of us took a penny until 1967 when we actually scheduled airshows.

I remember we also had a problem with mosquitoes [the insect variety] in those early days. So in true Old Rhinebeck tradition we went for the straightforward approach: Cole laid out some old bags of insecticide that had been lying around for a while, got us to slit them open, and he started up the Sopwith Snipe and blew the bags, insecticide and the mosquitoes to kingdom come!

Stanley Segalla, who is still a regular part of the weekend shows with his flying farmer routine, has many stories of the early years to tell:

I was flying my Piper Cub in about 1958–59 and saw three or four planes on the ground so I landed. Boy what a rough field. Cole introduced himself – he was working on the SPAD at the time, and said, 'Go around and lift the tail for me will ya.' I went round the back and grabbed a hold of it. I thought it was tied down, I couldn't move it. Cole started to laugh; that tail weighs about 450 lb. That's how we got acquainted all right.

We started flying together and every Sunday we took bags of lime up and put a tire in the center of the field and each put fifty cents in the pot. Then we'd drop the bags and the closest would win the pot. In those days three or four dollars was enough to pay for the gas.

They would also take up ten-foot-long streamers and throw them out of the cockpit to see how many they could catch on the leading edges of their wings.

Cole had it tough starting off here. He did an awful lot of work and I don't think people will realize how much for many years to come. It was his dream to show the aeroplanes flying, not to set them in a hangar. He could very easily have set up a museum and charged so much a head but that wasn't what he wanted. His dream was to fly the aeroplanes as they were when they were built so he built them back to the original spec. With the Avro 504K I told him that he ought to fit brakes but no, they never had brakes so he wasn't going to fit any now. He wouldn't change his mind even though these old timers are very difficult to land, especially here at Old Rhinebeck. But every aeroplane he built he flew himself before he would let anyone else fly it. He was a good pilot, a good mechanic and he just devoted his time to working on his aeroplanes. Actually I think Cole has done more for aviation than Amelia Earhart or Lindbergh or any one of 'em.

Most great characters have a stubborn streak, and Cole was no exception on some occasions. Stanley Segalla remembers the time when he was starting the Fokker Triplane for Cole:

I saw one of the valve springs fly off and I told him to shut the engine off, but he said, 'No! The centrifugal weight will hold it.' Well he took off, so I got in my Cub and followed. Cole force-landed in a lot about four miles away. I didn't say anything to him, he just jumped in my Cub and I brought him back to the field. Next day he went back in the car to find the Triplane, but couldn't find it from ground level, so in the end he had to jump into an aeroplane to find out where it was.

LEFT:
Pretty she ain't, but the Curtiss Jenny (a corruption of the JN prefix) was the most widely used trainer for American and Canadian pilots; it is estimated that 95 per cent of them learned to fly on military Jennys.

BELOW:
The backdrop of the Catskill mountains makes a great setting for any air-to-air photo session, but with Old Rhinebeck's Jenny in the viewfinder it could easily be a scene from the 1920s when the lone barnstormer would land in a field hoping to pick up some fare-paying passengers as he criss-crossed the country.

ABOVE:
Dick King, one of Cole Palen's longest-serving pilots, flies their oldest original airworthy American aeroplane. This Curtiss Jenny, dating from around 1917, is powered by an American-built Wright 150 hp Hispano-Suiza making it officially a very rare JN-4H survivor. The more common power plant was the 90 hp Curtiss OX-5, which still powers the majority of the handful that remain airworthy today.

OPPOSITE:
Unlimited visibility, clear skies, a good forecast and a vintage Jenny; what more could a pilot ask for?

ABOVE:
Bill King checks the Jenny's 'Hisso' engine for a suspected fuel leak.

RIGHT:
When Cole bought his job lot of six aeroplanes, the SPAD XIII was probably his greatest restoration challenge. Having built it, he then had to learn to fly it with only his limited experience on low-powered tail-draggers to that date.

Kay Bainbridge, widow of Gordon Bainbridge, a school teacher who was a very great friend and collaborator of Cole Palen's, takes up the story:

Gordon was building a large model of an SE5a for my son when a young fellow in school told him, 'Mr Bainbridge there is a fella out right near us and he has aeroplanes just like the one you're building.' 'There is? OK, tonight I'm going to take you home from school and we're going to find it,' replied Gordon. Thankfully he did find the strip, met Cole and they became very good friends. My husband did silk screen printing and made posters. Cole thought it was a ball and we soon had aeroplane posters all over the place. At the first airshow they said OK, Gordon you are the announcer, and he did that until the shows got larger and too much for him. He also became Cole's main restoration collaborator.

We worked on the movie *Those Magnificent Men in their Flying Machines*, we re-covered the Blériot and worked on the rusted gear. I also helped with woodworking, scraping off encrusted castor oil, and Gordon and I rib-stitched together one on one side and one on the other. Cole and friends went on a thirteen-week road tour around the US, flying their aeroplanes at special events to publicize the film.

In all we had fifteen of Cole's aeroplanes go through our house for refurb or rebuild and three of our own. We had a two-car garage, 24 ft × 24 ft, with the 'shop' above; a boom could be swung out above this opening so that fuselages and pieces of aircraft could be got in and out easily. The last one we brought out here in 1991 was the Nieuport 11 Bébé, but before that Gordon rebuilt the Snipe after its forced landing; he rebuilt it in a year and we put a new Bentley engine in it so it could have flown again. The SPAD XIII rebuild took two years. Boy that was something else! Gordon restored a Taylorcraft and built a Jodel and a Baby Great Lakes from scratch too.

After the Sopwith Snipe crashed we had 5,000 people here. There had been a radio spot by a gas company which said, 'Fill up your tank and if you're looking for a place to go – go to Old Rhinebeck Aerodrome.' We really couldn't handle that amount of people – cars were parked a mile and a half to the end of the road and then further down Route 9. That was an unusual one and it scared everybody.

Jim Hare, Old Rhinebeck's current Museum and Airshow Coordinator, worked for Cole for many years:

Cole's attic was full of his aircraft records and log books, shelves and shelves of aircraft parts and rare engine parts, flight instruments still in their original oil cloth wrappings and aeronautical journals from way back. The attic was so full of these treasures that it was difficult to move between them. But tragedy struck the Palen's Old Rhinebeck home in January 1983 while they were away at their Florida home. The entire house burnt down. I saw him shortly after he had received the phone call. I asked him what was wrong. He just turned and said dejectedly, 'The house burned down!' Everything went, nothing was salvageable, including his treasure trove in the attic. Cole's quote of 'what's gone is gone' summed up his philosophy of life.

The house was rebuilt and stands to this day near the aerodrome's main gate.

Another incident which would have knocked most people sideways happened when Cole was roading his original Aeromarine 39B on a trailer down to his winter base in Florida. He reckoned that someone had thrown a lighted

cigarette butt into the aircraft's fuselage, and fire completely destroyed it.

As the years went by the collection expanded and began to include antique vehicles and more vintage aviation memorabilia. Dick King told me that when Cole felt the need to build a new aeroplane to star in his shows he would often go to where an original could be found. Whether it be the Musée de l'Air in Paris or the Shuttleworth Collection in England, his technique was the same. He took thick paper with him to rub over the fittings, and would then make a note of the gauge of the metal and the size of fasteners. He would also take with him a big 'C' clamp with movable fingers to measure the width of the fuselage at one-foot intervals. To get the airfoil shape right he would take a few dimensions and lots of photographs. It was simple to him, but the rest of us can only marvel at what he achieved.

Cole began to ponder the future. In the 1970s he started the work that would perpetuate his dream. He wanted to ensure that his collection would always be presented to the public, and by the early 1990s, before his stroke, Cole had definite plans in place for the aerodrome's future.

Cole Palen's passing, on 7 December 1993, introduced the next chapter of Old Rhinebeck Aerodrome. In his Will he gifted two of his original (from his original six) World War One aircraft – a 1918 Sopwith Snipe to the National Air and Space Museum at the Smithsonian Institute, and a 1918 SPAD XIII to the United States Air Force Museum in Dayton, Ohio. The rest of his collection was given to the world through the creation of two non-profit-making educational corporations – the Rhinebeck Aerodrome Museum and Old Rhinebeck Aerodrome Air Shows. It was Cole's dream to have his lifelong collection available to the public, to create a proper museum and ensure that his vintage aircraft continued to fly.

The new status saved the collection from predators, for as soon as Cole's death was announced the telephones at Old Rhinebeck became red hot with potential buyers asking which aeroplanes were up for grabs. The insensitivity of these people puts the human race to shame – those good people manning the Rhinebeck phones were in shock, they were mourning their leader and guru, their best friend had just died. But on the other hand Cole's friends must have been very relieved and proud to tell these people, politely, 'to go away, the aeroplanes can't be sold, they belong to the nation'.

Now Rhinebeck Aerodrome Museum and Old Rhinebeck Aerodrome Air Shows have seven people serving on the Board of Trustees and an advisory committee comprising a further ten members. There is a team of five full-time personnel year round including the three key men who run the place full time: Jim Hare, Museum and Airshow Coordinator; Ken Cassens, Director of Maintenance; and Gene DeMarco, Flight Operations/ Museum Coordinator. During the summer months another five helpers are added, and on airshow days they employ a further fifteen part-timers to keep the spectators fed, watered and entertained.

LEFT:
Cole Palen was a real showman, and apart from his flying exploits he had a wicked sense of humor and took on the role of Eloc Nelap (Cole Palen spelt backwards), the famous World War One fighter ace. Introduced to the crowd with a lady on each arm he wore full make-up with an extremely red nose, and when questioned by the announcer about his twenty-six conquests during the war, he is confused! The announcer is talking about victories in the air but the doddering ninety-year-old Mr Nelap is stuttering out an altogether different story of conquests. So convincing was he that many of the spectators really believed that Cole Palen was a ninety-year-old who walked with the aid of sticks.

BELOW:
After a successful test flight in the Sopwith Dolphin, Cole leaves his team to top up the radiator of the 180 hp Hispano-Suiza engine and heads off to see what has been going on in his absence.

Not all of the restoration work takes place at Old Rhinebeck. Dan Taylor, who flies some of ORA's pioneer aircraft, was about to start building an Avro Triplane at his home in New Canaan, Connecticut, fifty miles away from the aerodrome. He shelved this plan after he was asked if he would like to restore Cole's repro of a Santos Dumont Demoiselle. The remains of this early Palen repro were found in Cole's Florida facility. This Demoiselle, together with a Curtiss Pusher, were Cole's first ever attempts at reproduction and were built at his parents' home. Dan is trying to make the aircraft as authentic as possible using materials available at the turn of the century. The fuselage is made of bamboo poles bound with brass wire every foot for greater strength. The machine will be displayed with a two-cylinder air-cooled opposed engine, fitted just above the pilot's head.

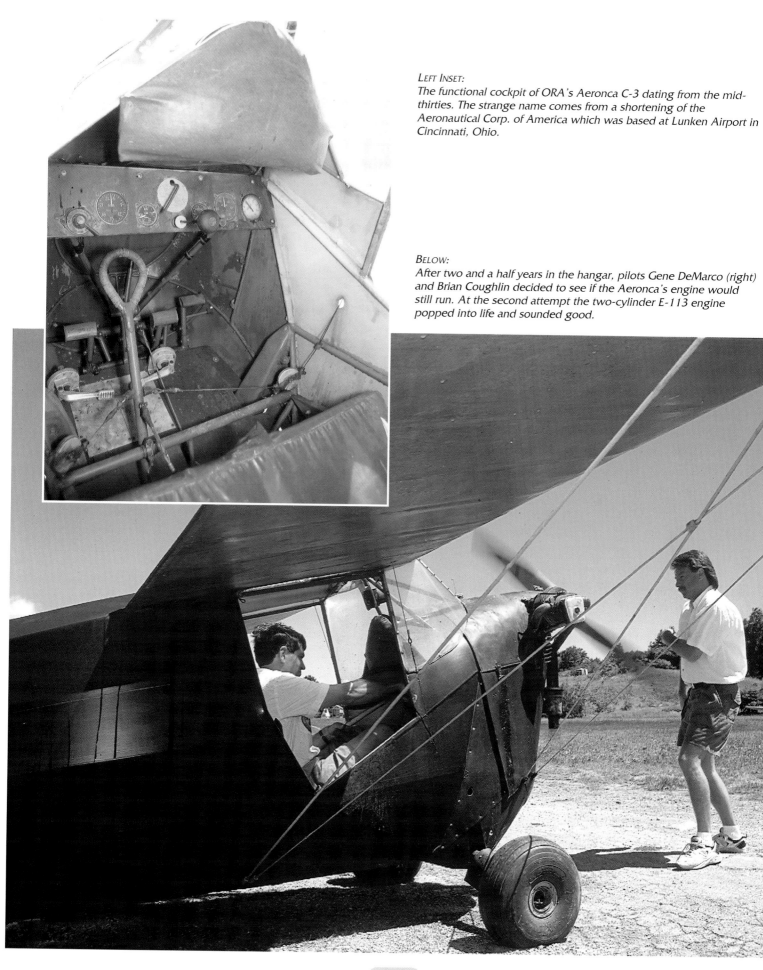

The functional cockpit of ORA's Aeronca C-3 dating from the mid-thirties. The strange name comes from a shortening of the Aeronautical Corp. of America which was based at Lunken Airport in Cincinnati, Ohio.

BELOW:
After two and a half years in the hangar, pilots Gene DeMarco (right) and Brian Coughlin decided to see if the Aeronca's engine would still run. At the second attempt the two-cylinder E-113 engine popped into life and sounded good.

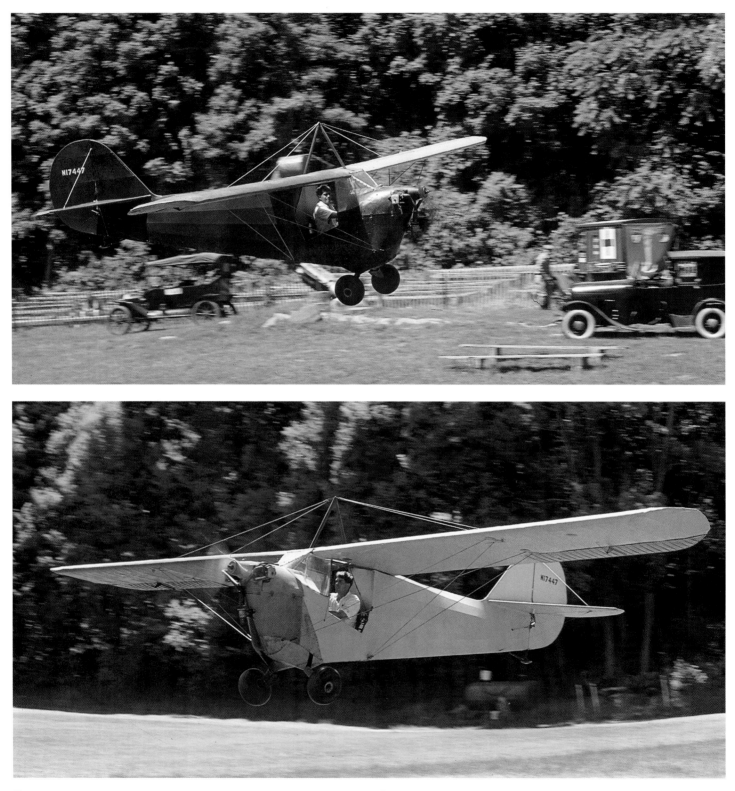

TOP:
After proving that the engine worked, the Aeronca was given a wash and fresh fuel was squirted into the tank. An early spectator on the crowd line asks if they're going to fly it? Even I wasn't sure what their plan was until Brian Coughlin taxied down to the end of the runway. Sure enough the engine is run up and this black and yellow grand-daddy of all Aeroncas flies on a short hop along the field for the benefit of early Show Day watchers.

BOTTOM:
It was an Aeronca C-3 that had the distinction of being the first aircraft ever to be flown off Cole's new runway at Old Rhinebeck back in the fifties. This aircraft is painted in black on one side of the aircraft and yellow on the other. The joke at Old Rhinebeck is that the aircraft was owned by two people and they couldn't agree a color scheme.

The entrance to Old Rhinebeck Aerodrome. Get there early before too many people have arrived to savor the tranquility of the place; watch the ground crews pushing and pulling the aeroplanes out of their old open-ended hangars as they are moved out to the flight line.

RIGHT:
Rita Palen (right) is pictured here with her sister Marion Weidner. They both still run the airfield shop on show days.

Old Rhinebeck Aerodrome as it was in 1997 after its runway widening program. The old runway has darker colored grass while the new lighter area (center bottom left) is where the hill used to be. Before the widening took place Old Rhinebeck's runway was very narrow; but its switchback is very much still there.

Dan Taylor attempts to start the Blériot XI's 35 hp 'Y'-type Anzani three-cylinder engine. The Blériot is named after the famous Frenchman Louis Blériot who was the first person to cross the English Channel in a heavier-than-air machine. That was back in 1909; it is still regarded as an incredible achievement even by today's airmen.

OPPOSITE PAGE:
Cole rebuilt this Blériot from some original parts given
to him by Mr Bill Champlin from Laconia, New
Hampshire, in the spring of 1952 at his parents' farm.
The parts didn't add up to much though: no wings,
no engine, no stabilizer and perhaps only one half of
the fuselage. Cole was pleased though, for the parts
he had were original, most of the metal fittings were
intact, and the name plate was inscribed as No. 56.
The aircraft was moved to Stormville Airport in
October 1954 for final fitting, and the first post-
restoration flight took place about a month later.

RIGHT:
Two of Old Rhinebeck's pilots who specialize in flying
and maintaining the three airworthy pioneer aircraft
wait for the wind to die down. Looking a bit like
Orville and Wilbur Wright waiting for the right
moment to launch one of their early fliers are Karl
Erickson (left) and Dan Taylor. Karl is a full-time
restorer at a museum facility near Hudson, New York,
whereas Dan is part-time and earns a living as a disc
jockey.

BELOW:
Perfect conditions for a 'pioneer era aircraft' flying
session. It is close to sunset and there isn't a breath of
wind to upset the fragile Blériot XI dating from
1909/10. Karl Erickson is at the controls and he's
struggling to keep the nose of the aircraft down so
that he can keep the wing at the correct angle of
attack to maintain lift.

BELOW:
Karl Erickson has the Blériot's nose pitched down for the correct flying attitude and the engine is pulling well. Karl explained that when you start to hop these early machines you feel that you are at fifty feet and it's not until you've landed that the watching ground crew bring you down to earth with the news that the highest you got was ten to fifteen feet.

BOTTOM:
Dan Taylor tops up the Blériot's Anzani 35 hp 'Y'-type engine with motor oil. Overnight a different propeller was fitted to try to improve performance for the next day's flight. If anything the performance was even poorer, so it was back to the drawing board again.

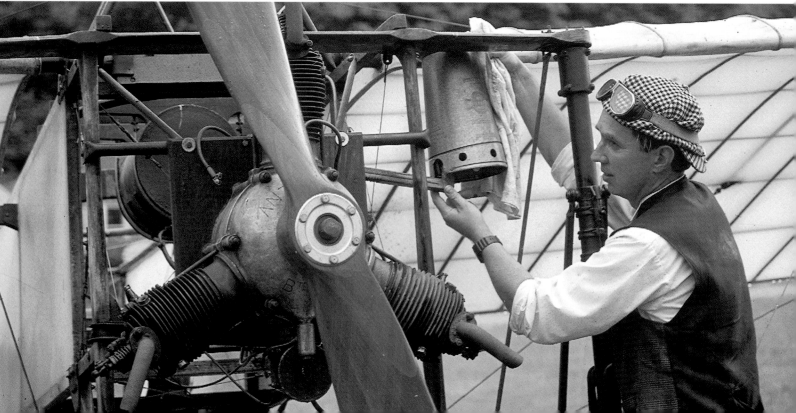

The Blériot XI's cockpit is very basic by today's standards but it's got all the required ingredients that today's pilot would recognize. The main difference, though, is that the control column operates the wing warping system (and not the ailerons as on a modern a/c) and you can see the rudder bar mounted on the floor. The metal tank is for the fuel. It is the proud boast at Old Rhinebeck that this aircraft is the oldest original aeroplane flying in the United States.

ABOVE:
Glenn Curtiss was a master American aircraft designer; right from the start most of his aeroplanes always looked as if they were going to achieve flight, unlike many of the other emerging types of that era. His Curtiss 'D' Pusher dates from around 1911. The beautiful ORA replica was built in 1976 and is powered by an original 1911 eight-cylinder 80 hp Hall Scott water-cooled engine which was obtained from the National Air and Space Museum. The view here is from the rear of the aircraft, and between the pilot and the prop is the radiator.

RIGHT:
The pilot of the Curtiss Pusher literally has his hands full when flying. The pilot seat has what appears to be a metal arm rest around it, but this is the method of moving the ailerons as the pilot leans left or right. Control wheel rotation works the rudder, the wheel fore and aft movement controls both forward and rear elevators, the pilot's right foot controls the throttle, while the center pedal is the front wheel friction brake and the left boot is for an emergency claw brake which digs into the ground as a last resort, and regarded as not very effective by the pilots.

BELOW:
A Sunday show scene as the crowd watch the dastardly Black Baron in his Fokker F.1 Triplane fly overhead. Not the machine that Rita found in her living room; this repro was built by Hank Palmer and Fred Wilgus (well-known restorers of early aircraft) in Florida. The designation F.1 instead of Dr.1 shows that the original Dr.1 would have been one of three pre-production aircraft. One went to von Richthofen, one to Fokker's Schwerin works and one to Werner Voss, for tests.

OPPOSITE:
A glorious day to go flying even if you are the evil Black Baron. There are of course no original Fokker Triplanes in existence today, but this repro was built using plans from one captured by the British during World War One. Only 320 Dr.1s were built, and I estimate the count of reproductions worldwide must be in the order of thirty to forty.

OPPOSITE:
Pictured with its twin Spandau 7.29 mm machine-guns which fired through the arc of the prop, the cockpit of the Dr. 1 is very basic, but practical.

BELOW:
A Triplane was the favorite mount of the Red Baron (Baron Manfred von Richthofen) too, but these original craft were known to break up in the air and were eventually withdrawn from operations. The Black Baron, however, has this magnificent reproduction with its modern 220 hp Continental radial engine to power his trusty mount. This engine gives far greater reliability, enabling the aircraft to be flown at airshows away from home.

Even a Triplane which 'belongs' to the evil Black Baron has to have a
wash before showtime. The frowning face painted on the cowling
was first used by the German ace Werner Voss.

The Triplane, or 'Driedekker' as they are known by the Germans, is ready and waiting to carry the Black Baron on his quest to kidnap Trudy Truelove. One unusual aspect of the Dr.1 design is that it has no bracing wires between the upper, mid and lower wings. The entire set of wings is cantilevered to support the airplane's flying surfaces without wires.

ABOVE:
Designed to be entered in the 1914 Gordon Bennett Cup Race, the Nieuport 11 was quickly pressed into service in World War One and armed with a Lewis gun (seen here visible just above the top wings). It has a very good rate of climb and excellent maneuverability. This aircraft set the style for the entire series of 'strutters' that followed.

RIGHT:
Pilot Gene DeMarco 'runs-up' the 'Bébé,' as the Nieuport 11 was affectionately known. In the background is Gene's Howard DGA 15P. The initials DGA stand for Damn Good Airplane.

Nieuport 11s equipped the famous American volunteer group The Lafayette Escadrille. This machine is painted in the colors of Victor Chapman, a local American hero who flew with the Lafayette and was sadly the first American pilot to lose his life during World War One.

A closer look at the Sopwith Camel's original 160 hp Gnôme rotary engine.

SHOWTIME

I t's a blazing hot July weekend and my first Old Rhinebeck show for seven years. I have waited far too long to see the greatest aviation show on earth again. It's also my first show since the sad loss of Cole back in 1993. What will it be like?

Changes have been made at Old Rhinebeck, some of which have been undertaken on the advice of the FAA. Not the least is the fact that in 1992 the FAA insisted the airshow display line be pushed back 500 feet from the crowd line – this meant that the aircraft had to display over the trees making it even more dangerous for the pilots, especially those flying the rotary-engined machines which are more likely to suffer a sudden silence up front.

In the winter and spring of 1996/97 the trustees decided that the safest way to achieve this was to widen Old Rhinebeck's famous dog-leg runway at the north end to twice its original width. This enormous job, which meant blasting out a hill of solid rock eighty feet high by 400 feet across covered in trees, plus another ridge 300 feet long by fifty feet wide, was completed just in time for the start of the 1997 season at a cost of around $100,000. Interestingly, Oak Cookingham, the founder of the company from Red Hook who carried out the work, helped Cole bulldoze out his original runway in the late 1950s and early 1960s.

Brian Coughlin's Stearman PT-17 (it actually belongs to his wife) takes part in the balloon bursting competitions and bomber raids which are a feature of Old Rhinebeck shows.

The grand-daddy of all Stearmans was designed by Mac Stuart and Lloyd Stearman with their A.70 training biplane design from 1933. The family tree continues with the A.73 (Lloyd Stearman's last design) to the PT-13 and eventually the PT-17, which was ordered in huge quantities by the US military for World War Two pilot training by both Air Force and Navy.

At the show, I stand waiting for the lone parachutist trailing the Stars and Stripes to descend; he is accompanied from the ground by the national anthem played on a flute. His touchdown is timed to the final note. During this stillness I can almost hear Cole's voice back in 1990 telling me how the shows came about:

We began by holding an airshow on the last Sunday of each month during the season. The shows were still very formal, with an announcer, and the aircraft performed one at a time. All services were volunteered and very often the show crews outnumbered the audience. We used to buy in cans of drinks and sell them for the same price, trusting the spectators to throw the right money into an ice bucket, just so that they could have something to drink on a hot day – we had no idea how to make a profit.

The ideas that made Old Rhinebeck what it is today came very gradually. We all thought something was lacking and then came the ideas which make my show different from any other airshow in the world. We decided we would tell a story during shows with a good guy, a bad guy and a pretty girl enacting a story of love and deceit played out against a backdrop of dogfights and aerial bombardment with World War One aeroplanes. Thus was born the Black Baron of Old Rhinebeck, Sir Percy Goodfellow and Trudy Truelove.

Suddenly, 'Okay boys and girls, showtime approaches' roars from the speakers and brings me back to the present day. Jim Hare (who is the commentator too) is up in his tower and greeting the crowd at the start of the two-hour Saturday show which majors on the early pioneer aircraft. But first comes the fashion show. Volunteers from the audience, dressed in costumes from the Victorian, Edwardian and 1920s periods, are introduced to the spectators while parading across the stage before being driven around the airfield in the museum's beautiful antique vehicles.

Meanwhile, Bill King in his DH Tiger Moth, Gene DeMarco in his Stampe SV.4b and Dick King in the Great Lakes have taken off to gain altitude before they are required on stage at 1,000 feet for the start of the 'Delsey Dive'. Rolls of toilet tissue are thrown from their cockpits, and amidst great encouragement from Jim Hare and the crowd alike, they see how many cuts they can make in the tissue as the roll rapidly descends towards the earth. Funny, when I went to school the numbers went 1, 2, 3, 4, 5; Old Rhinebeck's version seems more like 1, 2, 5, 6, 8. While the pilots compete the commentator could do with an official scorer. No one really cares about the score though as it is great to see these lovely old aeroplanes having an excuse to cavort about the sky.

I soon realized after my second Saturday show that no two are exactly the same. But somewhere in between Officer O'Malley falling off a wing and the Keystone Cops chasing a convict who pinches an aeroplane, you see some wonderful aircraft take to the skies, including, if the weather is calm

enough, the Blériot XI, Hanriot and Curtiss Model D Pusher, dating from 1909 to 1911. The Blériot is an original machine while the Hanriot and the Curtiss Pusher are reproductions. The Pusher, however, is powered by an original 1911 80 hp Hall Scott engine while the Hanriot is pulled along by a 50 hp Franklin dating from 1939. Today's Old Rhinebeck pilots still marvel at the skills required by the early pilots, who often had to teach themselves to fly in these very fragile and unstable craft.

One of Old Rhinebeck's pioneer aircraft, the Demoiselle, can be seen flying if the weather is calm enough during the Saturday shows. This modern metal version of Santos Dumont's 1909 aeroplane has a 65 hp Continental engine. The original would have had a 17–25 hp Dutheil-Chalmers or early equivalent fitted. Santos Dumont, a Brazilian who weighed in at a mere 90 lb, was able to get airborne on far less horsepower than heavier pilots. He made the first officially observed flight in history – a flight of 722 feet in 1906. In 1907 he designed the Demoiselle using bamboo, wood and linen in its main construction, and generously made the plans public property.

The Sunday shows are really something else. The cast wear make-up and costumes depicting the period, and the nearest you can get to describing this ninety-minute saga of love and mayhem would be a comparison with the early silent movies, but brought up to date with the sound fully turned up and, of course, in glorious color. To add to the mayhem, antique cars, motor bikes, an old ambulance and an original World War One Renault tank are employed to keep the action moving on the ground. It is known as the 'craziness' or the 'silliness' amongst the team and the spectators love it. But the real stars of the show are the aeroplanes. As Cole told me: 'We could do the whole show with Piper Cubs but the reason for whatever success we have is that we fly pretty, authentic aeroplanes and people love to see 'em fly.'

I'm relieved to see, as I await my first Sunday show, that the bad Black Baron of Rhinebeck lives on – I've just seen him applying a fake scar to his cheek. Earlier at briefing he had lost it but thankfully managed to locate it before showtime. The crowd are taking their seats on the bleachers (wooden tiered plank seats) ready for the off. They have examined the show aircraft lined up at the boundary fence, visited the gift shop and the 1918 rest rooms, eaten their hot dogs and taken or booked a flight in the New Standard D-25 biplane. Now they want to see the fun, and so do I.

I was to experience the first part of the show from the air strapped into the front cockpit of Bill King's DH 82a Tiger Moth. Along with Gene DeMarco and his Stampe, Dick King

in the Great Lakes 2-T-1MS and Brian Coughlin in his Stearman PT-17, we line up in formation for a low run, then pull up and break formation for the start of the balloon bursting competition. The pilots are all pitted against each other and I find out afterwards that if there is a dead heat between them the spectators get to decide the tie-break by judging which is the best landing. From the cockpit, of course, we can't hear Jim's commentary, just the noise of the Tiger's Gipsy Major engine as we climb and dive trying to burst the ground-launched balloons with our prop. The balloons are very difficult to spot from the air, never mind hitting one. If you've ever tried clay pigeon shooting and thought that was difficult, just imagine doing it from a vibrating and fast-moving platform. Most surprising of all to me was the fact that you could actually hear the balloon burst from the Tiger's cockpit. Our tally was two balloons and a couple of near misses on this occasion, which as far as I was concerned meant that we had won this day's competition, – I didn't even see the balloons and thought it was a real achievement that we had managed to hit any at all!

Back on the ground, I and a thousand others are reloading cameras as the show is taking off rapidly. I wondered if anyone from the current cast of characters would take over the mantle of Cole Palen's comic World War One ace Eloc Nelap, but I guess out of respect or for sheer timing no one could follow Cole on this one; he was brilliant as he told the story of his conquests.

OPPOSITE:
Poor Officer O'Malley was just chasing a convict. Next thing he knows he's tied to the bracing wires of the Stampe SV-4B as it takes off during a Saturday show. How was he to know the convict was going to steal an aeroplane? It's a tough life.

BELOW:
Gene DeMarco's Stampe SV-4B 'Lucky 7' (foreground), Brian Coughlin's PT-17 Stearman and Old Rhinebeck's Great Lakes 2-T-1MS put on a show for my camera above the Hudson Valley's magnificent scenery.

Wonderful veteran aeroplanes such as the Curtiss Jenny and the Fokker trio of Triplane, D.VII and D.VIII fill the skies over Rhinebeck as they do battle with the Sopwith Camel, Avro 504K and Nieuport Bébé from World War One. They fly overhead as the story of Sir Percy Goodfellow and Trudy Truelove unfolds on the ground. That is until the bad Black Baron interrupts Sir Percy's birthday party, hands him a stick of dynamite, and abducts his fiancée. The scheming Black Baron and his cohorts tie her to the interplane wing struts of the Jenny and carry her aloft – not the real Trudy, of course; she has been switched for a realistic dummy. 'Boo and hiss, shake your fists, here comes the Black Baron again,' Jim yells to the crowd. 'Oh my, I've never seen him do anything that bad before,' he gasps as Trudy Truelove (well, the dummy) is thrown out in mid-flight from about 500 feet. The crowd are loving it but some of the smaller children aren't so sure at this point. Caring parents assure them that it's not for real, but they still don't seem too assured.

Over in the village – a row of painted wooden mock-up buildings on the far side of the runway – Madame Fifi has been taking a bath at the Hotel de Paree. Now only at Old Rhinebeck could someone fire a rocket, shot from a tuba, and blow the front off. She is revealed in pale pink pantaloons standing in the bath and her piercing scream can be heard across the aerodrome without the aid of microphones!

For many, this ride in the D-25 biplane, recognized as the king of barnstormers, is their first ever taste of open-cockpit flying, but you can guarantee they will all come back with huge grins across their faces. For as the tee-shirt boasts, 'I survived my ride in the D-25'.

The bombs go off and the story unfolds, but the good guy wins in the end as Trudy Truelove finally blows up the Black Baron who is stretchered away in a vintage ambulance amidst boos and hisses, and some cheers from the crowd, depending on whose side they're on.

Somewhere in the middle of all this we are treated to an amazing 'flying farmer' routine by Stanley Segalla. Now well-known for this routine Stanley 'One Shot' Segalla was for many years the pilot who dispatched the Black Baron (then Cole Palen) once a week with Le Prieur rockets fired from the interplane struts of Rhinebeck's Avro 504K. During a quiet moment before the show Stanley described his show-stopping routine which he has been performing for over twenty-five years. When I met him he was just getting over a broken pelvis from an accident five weeks earlier when he fell off a box while working on his Piper PA-11 Cub. The show that we're about to see today was his first since that accident. It's the way that Stanley works his act into the show that gives it just that bit more believability than just a straightforward crazy flying act. He works the crowd through the commentator for over an hour before he even takes to the air:

I make out that I want a flight home to my farm just over the hill because I've got to help my wife get the hay in. The announcer suggests that I've been drinking cider and have become such a nuisance that he says to the crowd, 'Just bear with us, folks, while we fly the farmer home.' Once in the Cub I take off without the pilot and leave the commentator with all the explaining to do to the crowd.

The early evening sun shines on the wings of the New Standard D-25 as it takes a full load of four fare-paying passengers sitting two by two and sharing just a lap strap between two. In the background are the Great Lakes 2-T-1MS, the Stampe SV-4 and the PT-17

'I take off over the trees and disappear so that they all think I've crashed. I've got a clothes line aboard which is supposed to be Madame Fifi's so I throw it out and the crowd can see it on my return to the field. I can just imagine the announcer winding up the crowd with, 'Boy is she going to be mad again.' I fly back over again with my leg hanging out and hollering for help. I set off my smoke bomb and do three loops at 300 feet, if the wind is right, then I go back up and do a reverse Cuban eight and another to bring me back in front of the crowd, then as I fly away from them I go into a hammerhead.

All this in his 85 hp Cub, which is not regarded as an aerobatic aeroplane.

Stanley's show continues with the crowd not at all sure if they are witnessing a real emergency or part of Old Rhinebeck's renowned craziness. From 900 feet he enters a spin appearing to pull out at the last moment. Then a run down the runway at fifty feet and at 110 mph he climbs and rolls the Cub. Back at 800 feet with the door open he keeps hollering 'Help, Help!' He throttles back and at about 30 mph just drifts around and slides sideways. If the wind is right the Cub will actually back up. After gaining some forward momentum again Stanley switches off the engine and flies a dead stick, one wheel landing with just enough inertia to stop and pick up his hat from his starting point. He starts the engine again and taxies along the crowd line and with the tail wheel off the ground he sits applauding the crowd with both hands. When the spectators see this they all realize that they have seen the master at work and witnessed some very special flying.

Cole Palen's hunch for knowing what the public wanted and giving it to them is undoubtedly the secret of Old Rhinebeck's appeal to the public. You feel as if you have been time-warped back into an easier age when the private pilot could pull his aeroplane out of his barn and fly without restriction. I imagine the family atmosphere amongst the helpers, pilots and cast being reminiscent of a band of traveling theatricals centuries ago.

Cole was definitely a member of the team; he would be hard at work most mornings from six a.m. until late, and some evenings he could be seen flying his aircraft models until sundown. He would make sure that he and his team got a couple of days off each week to refresh themselves for the next weekend. During a show Cole was just as likely to be found warming up a plane to enable another pilot to make a quick getaway during the fast and furious show as he was flying his magnificent machines himself. 'When he died he must have left a gaping hole in the fabric of Old Rhinebeck,' I said to John Barker, who played the Black Baron and was Chief Pilot under Cole for many years, and also a very close friend. He told me of the memorial that was held at Old Rhinebeck at the first public show of the season in 1994:

After Cole's stroke earlier in 1993 he had made such a good recovery that we thought he might get his license back and be flying with us again. But it wasn't to be, and as Cole died in Florida we felt that we hadn't been able to mourn him properly. Six weeks before this Gordon Bainbridge had died tragically, so we'd lost two of the main players in a very short time.

We decided that on the first show day after Cole's death [around six months later] we would have a memorial flypast in front of an ordinary airshow crowd. We explained in advance to them that this was a very special day to all of the aerodrome's faithful.

What a send-off we gave him. A lone piper stood on the hill and played 'Taps' as we flew a missing man formation with six of our World War One aeroplanes. When we got level with the piper I flew off the formation in Cole's Fokker Triplane and hit the black smoke release. It was the most moving and difficult occasion that I have ever attended; there wasn't a dry eye on the field.

As soon as we had landed we started our usual show with a bang. This is how Cole would have wanted it, 'on with the show'.

Ken Cassens pilots the D-25 as it takes off with another load of intrepid passengers. Trips last about fifteen minutes (cost $30 per person in 1997) and take you out towards the mighty Hudson river. The scenery is wonderful, and so is the flight, and there is always the chance that you will see more of Rhinebeck's aircraft while airborne.

The Fokker D.VII is pulled gently from its hangar to be lined up ready for the show. This repro was made by Cole Palen; the original was designed by Fokker S P Werke's talented designer Rheinhold Platz in January 1918. It was his most successful aircraft design to date. In the background can be seen the open-fronted airfield hangars containing an Avro 504K and a PT-17 Stearman.

Fokker D.VII pilot Ken Cassens switches on the smoke to accentuate the climbing ability of this 200 hp Mercedes-powered machine; they were strong, fast and maneuverable. These high-flying German fighters gained a great deal of respect from Allied pilots. When they reached combat in July 1918 they accounted for the downing of more than 275 Allied aircraft in a very short time.

ABOVE:
A clear blue sky shows off the Fokker D.VII a treat. This solid plane could take untold punishment and was greatly maneuverable at high altitude. So feared was it that the Allies stipulated that all of them were to be turned over to them under the terms of the Treaty of Versailles. Anthony Fokker, however, managed to smuggle many back to his native Holland after the war to keep his business afloat.

LEFT:
White scarf flapping in the slipstream, Ken Cassens gets the Fokker D.VII's nose up. About a 1,000 of these very successful German planes were built.

RIGHT:
Old Rhinebeck's repro D.VII has a 200 hp in-line Mercedes engine and sounds great; originals, though, would have been fitted with slightly less powerful 180 hp Mercedes or 185 hp BMW engines.

BELOW:
The colorful paint scheme of the Fokker D.VII is painted with a scene from the Grimm Brothers' fairy tale 'The Seven Swabians', as was Gefreiter Scheutzel's craft. A picture of his original D.VII (OAW) 4649/18 aircraft has the scene emblazoned on both fuselage sides, but the paint scheme has since been changed and the picture is on display in the Fokker aerodrome hangar. The lozenge camouflage paint scheme on both the top and underside of the wings is authentic from World War One.

Pictured at sunset, this Fokker D.VIII was built and is owned by ORA pilot Brian Coughlin and is flown regularly in Old Rhinebeck shows. This is the second D.VIII he's built; the first he sold to a collector in California, but he missed it so much that he built another. Like all operators of rotary-engined craft though, Brian tries to keep the amount of unnecessary engine time to an absolute minimum.

OPPOSITE:
Under its half cowling the Fokker D.VIII has a very zippy Gnôme Type N nine-cylinder rotary air-cooled engine; it operates at 1,350 rpm and weighs 290 lb. It was the last of the famous Gnôme line and was used in Nieuport 28 and Morane Saulnier fighters. The engine speed is controlled by cutting the ignition from 2 revolutions to fire each cylinder at full power to 4 revs, 8 revs and 16 revs.

LEFT:
A look at the underside of this magnificent Fokker D.VIII repro gives a good idea of the clean lines of this parasol-winged machine that was to appear too late in World War One to do real battle.

BELOW:
Silk scarf trailing, Brian Coughlin in his D.VIII streaks past the Piper Cub camera platform. As already mentioned this Fokker design is known as the D.VIII but of course it should have been called an E.VIII as 'E' stands for Eindekker, or one wing.

RIGHT:
With fingers in ears the 'crew' stand by as Brian Coughlin runs up the engine of his D.VIII prior to take-off. The sound of this beast's Gnôme 160 running up gives a new meaning to government health warnings on noise. Although the type was recalled from service in August 1918 it returned on 24 October of that year with properly constructed wings and attachment points and saw limited combat before the Armistice on the 11th hour of the 11th day of the 11th month in 1918.

BELOW:
Brian Coughlin (in shorts – foreground) steers his D.VIII from its hangar with the aid of the tractor, which is known as the 'tug', his wife and their dachshund. A German dog and a German aeroplane!

LEFT:
The swept wings of NC304Y are plain to see from this view, if you'll excuse the pun, and it is pictured with a home-built Great Lakes 2T-1R Speedster constructed and owned by Ed Hammerle from Cooperstown, New York. Ed, who helps out at Old Rhinebeck, spent fifteen years researching and building his 175 hp Ranger-powered aeroplane from plans dating from 1932. Versions of the Great Lakes and Baby Great Lakes have been built by various companies and individuals since the golden era, underlining how much these beautiful machines still mean to modern generations.

BELOW:
Pretty as a picture the Great Lakes 2T-1MS, NC304Y, serial number 191, dating from 1930, started life as a 2-T-1E powered with a four-cylinder in-line inverted ACE 'Cirrus Hi-Drive' engine of 95 hp. A change to a Menasco Pirate 125 hp makes it officially a 2T-1MS model. NC304Y was always a great favorite of Cole's and was used by the Great Lakes Aircraft Corporation in their 1930s advertisements, the aircraft's registration being clearly visible.

Although this Hanriot is a reproduction, the controls are similar to the original. At the grand age of fourteen, Monsieur Hanriot's son managed to master them and flying one of his dad's creations became the youngest pilot in Europe. The right stick controls the elevator by fore-and-aft movements, the huge vertical stick on the left controls the wing warping, either left or right. It takes an enormous effort by the pilot to pivot this control pole across his torso in an unnatural movement. The coupé button on the left stick can kill the engine for speed control.

ABOVE:
A determined and an almost smiling Bill King flies this reproduction Hanriot in the Saturday pioneer show. The type dates from 1910 but this copy has a 50 hp Franklin flat four engine dating from 1939. The machine was built by Cole and his friends at Old Rhinebeck.

LEFT:
The fuselage of the Hanriot is built using the same techniques as those used in racing skiffs resulting in a light but strong frame. This aircraft was built in the winter of 1974 from drawings and details appearing in Flight and other books on period aeroplane construction.

RIGHT:
Pilot Bill King is a wizard at making the Hanriot perform. Here he is persuading it to bank over Old Rhinebeck's back lot village, so showing it off at its best angle for photographers in the crowd.

BELOW:
Helpers steady the craft as the pilot straps in ready to take the Hanriot for a short flight. The pilot's technique for mounting this machine is a bit strange to say the least: first get a leg-up from the ground crew, straddle the fuselage with a leg either side, draw your legs up under your chin and waggle forward on your bottom before dropping in over the back of the seat.

A sunset flight on a calm clear evening and from this angle the Hanriot appears to be above the treetops. But this is something the pilots never attempt to do with these early aircraft as any turbulence could quickly change their flight plan!

It was great to see this immaculate 230 hp Wright-powered Pitcairn PA-7 Mailwing arrive for the Golden Biplane fly-in at Old Rhinebeck. It was an even greater pleasure to meet the pilot and owner Mr Stephen Pitcairn, whose father Mr Harold F. Pitcairn had designed and built these beautiful mail and sport planes. Dating from 1927, about 150 of them were built. Stephen, who is obviously very proud of his family's aviation history, owns four more airworthy Mailwings, one PA-5, one PA-6, another PA-7 and one PA-8, as well as a PCA-2 Autogyro. Another of his family's Pitcairn Autogyros has been presented to the EAA Museum at Oshkosh.

ABOVE:
A pair of Fleet biplanes dating from around 1930 arrived for the fly-in and joined up with the DH Tiger Moth photo ship. The blue and yellow machine painted up in 'Roosevelt Flying School' colors is a Fleet Model 2 powered by a five-cylinder Kinner B5 radial of 125 hp. It is owned by Gene Briener, based at Bermudeian Valley, Pennsylvania, and flown here by John K. Machamer from Gettysburg, Pennsylvania. The red and white machine is a Fleet model 16B hauled along by a Kinner K.5 of 125 hp (note the different fin shape) and is owned and flown by Sandy Brown.

LEFT:
Over seventy de Havilland DH-82A Tiger Moths are now based in the US, so the sight of two in formation near Old Rhinebeck is not as rare as it used to be.

Ed Hammerle wings away from the photo plane in his home-built Great Lakes 2T-1R Speedster, heading for home about eighty miles north-west of Old Rhinebeck.

ABOVE:

Bill King lands in his DH 82a Tiger Moth. The aircraft carries the false British registration of G-ACDA. The first Tiger flew in 1931 and originally had a 120 hp Gipsy III inverted in-line engine which was subsequently changed to a 130 hp Gipsy Major. Over the years around 7,300 were built in England, Canada, Australia and New Zealand. Bill and his Tiger regularly take part in Old Rhinebeck shows performing the Delsey Dive and balloon bursting feats, amongst other things. He and his Tiger also acted as my camera platform for a lot of the air-to-air sorties featured in this book. Thanks Bill!

BELOW:

Probably the leading British fighter type of World War One, the Sopwith Camel destroyed more enemy aircraft than any other Allied type – some 980. This reproduction, built by Cole Palen in 1990, is complete with a 160 hp Gnôme engine and two Vickers machine-guns which would have been synchronized to fire through the airscrew arc in an original machine. The guns were partially enclosed in a hump-like fairing that gave rise to the 'Camel' nickname which was eventually officially recognized.

RIGHT:
The wind rushes past as the Sopwith Camel takes to the skies. In its flying qualities this type proved to be completely different to its more docile forebears. In the hands of a competent pilot it was incredibly maneuverable, but it had its drawbacks for the fledgling pilot and many mistakes were made by the poorly trained young men who were required to fly it after only a few hours' instruction.

OPPOSITE:
The neat but basic cockpit of Old Rhinebeck's Sopwith Camel.

BELOW:
The 'chocks' are in but helpers hang on grimly to the Camel's wings as it runs up in preparation for take-off. Behind the castor oil smoke cloud the Fokker D.VII waits to line up.

OPPOSITE TOP:
The Camel's 160 hp Gnôme rotary creates a 'fog' of castor oil smoke over its pilot and wingman as it prepares for take-off.

OPPOSITE BELOW:
Pilot Brian Coughlin administers a pre-show shower to spruce up the Sopwith Camel. In the background visiting airshow aircraft start to arrive including this Cessna Bird Dog. On the left are two Great Lakes biplanes. On the bench is Tom Dietricht and his gang of restorers who have driven from Canada two weeks running to attend the weekend shows.

BELOW:
The end of another show and Gene DeMarco clambers down from the cockpit of the Sopwith Camel. The aircraft will be pushed to within a foot of the crowd-line barrier so that the public can smell as well as see these wonderful machines at close quarters.

The start of the Stanley Segalla 'Flying Farmer' routine. The guy chasing the Piper Cub is supposed to be the 'pilot-in-charge', but he soon gets left behind in the chaos that ensues.

LEFT:
The maneuver that regularly brings the house down at Old Rhinebeck's airshows. To show his incredible control over his Piper PA-11 Cub, Stanley Segalla applauds the crowd with both hands off the control stick.

BELOW:
Landing his Cub on two wheels would be too easy and not very eye-catching, so Stanley the 'Flying Farmer' touches down on one.

*Ladies from the crowd who have taken part in the fashion show are
treated to a drive in the collection's vintage vehicles. A 1909 open-
top Renault leads the cavalcade.*

LEFT:
A rocket man gets loose and streaks across the field, usually managing to blow up Madame Fifi's place, just across the runway.

BELOW:
Oh my! Sir Percy's in danger. He gets easily confused you see and the bad Black Baron has taken advantage yet again. He's put a cone over Sir Percy's head and asked him to hold something for him. I suggest we all move back a few paces.

RIGHT:
The worst has happened, the Black Baron has kidnapped Trudy Truelove and mayhem ensues.

BELOW:
If memory serves me right this is part of the Saturday show and the cops, led by Officer O'Malley, in a 1916 Studebaker police car, are chasing an escaped convict.

LEFT:
'Come on you guys, what is going on out there?' and 'Holy smokes, what the heck is all that?' yells commentator Jim Hare above the din of explosions and a runway covered in black smoke, as the crazy events of a Sunday show unfold.

BELOW:
Bob Tator, seen here chauffeuring fashion show volunteers, is a long-time helper at Old Rhinebeck. He's seen it all from the beginning and still loves being involved in the shows; he loves cars and motorcycles too.

ABOVE:
More fashion show participants wait for a ride; a favorite is this beautiful bright yellow 1914 Ford model T Speedster.

RIGHT:
The Hotel de Paree gets a direct hit every Sunday and guess who's in the bath at the time? Yep! You've guessed it, poor old Madame Fifi.

LEFT:
Dave King is taking the part of the Black Baron at this show and boy does he look a nasty piece of work! Earlier at briefing he'd lost his false scar, but nobody seemed to want to help him find it.

BELOW:
If you're into tanks more than aeroplanes then this is the highlight of the show for you. An original 1917 Renault tank firing off some very noisy blanks gets involved in the plot.

Karl Erickson is fully airborne in the Curtiss 'D' Pusher. After a couple of hops down the field Karl will try out the Blériot for the Saturday crowd. I have never seen anyone scramble so quickly from one to the other as Karl does; I'm still waiting for him to get tangled in all those wires, but I guess he's too clever for that.

OPPOSITE:
The Nieuport 11, nicknamed 'Bébé', is a very pretty baby in this color scheme. From this angle it also shows how much narrower the bottom wing is compared to the top.

ABOVE:
Starting the Blériot XI's Anzani three-cylinder engine gives a wonderful smell of warm oil. The trusty mechanic waits to make sure that the engine is catching well and then gets out of the way fast so that the pilot can see that he is clear.

OPPOSITE:
We're chasing the Black Baron in his Fokker F.1 Triplane. We've got him worried, he keeps looking over his shoulder. Aw! Who are we kidding, we're flying in the Tiger Moth and haven't got any guns. Come on Bill, let's get out of here before he turns nasty.

OPPOSITE TOP:
The Curtiss Jenny JN-4H in the hands of Dick King is a fundamental part of the airshows. It has been disassembled for the first time since 1966, this is for a re-cover. It will be painted to represent a post-World War One U.S. Navy Hispano-powered Jenny. See if you notice the difference when you visit Old Rhinebeck.

OPPOSITE BOTTOM:
You can hear the crowd gasp as they see Trudy hanging on to the Jenny's upper wing. You see the Black Baron has pinched the Jenny as well as Trudy. Well it's only a dummy, but it does look pretty realistic you've got to agree.

BELOW:
The aerodrome's British-built repro Avro 504K takes off on a mission in the hands of Ken Cassens.

BELOW TOP:
At the top of the hill from the car park you will find these three hangars which were built during 1963–64 and house (left to right) Pioneer, World War One and Lindbergh era aircraft; on the right is the new Museum Building.

BELOW BOTTOM:
From the air in the foreground is the new Museum Building, and center are the three older hangars. At the top of picture you can just make out the backs of the aerodrome hangars.

RESTORATION AND PRESERVATION

The Rhinebeck Aerodrome Museum, one of the two corporations set up by Cole Palen, maintains one of the largest collections of early aeroplanes, engines and related items in the world. Its collection also includes early automobiles and motorcycles. It features aeroplanes of historical significance from the Pioneer, World War One and Lindbergh eras, spanning the period from the early 1900s to 1939. Over the years the aerodrome has collected, restored, re-created and/or flown more aeroplanes from the first thirty years of aviation than any other collection in the world.

Several restoration projects are always on-going and they have to be fitted around the routine maintenance needed to keep ORA's (Old Rhinebeck Aerodrome's) regular fleet of aircraft flying. The museum's current major project involves creating a reproduction of one of the most famous aeroplanes of all time, Lindbergh's *Spirit of St Louis*. Work was started by Cole Palen and Andy Keefe in the late 1980s and the collection's director of maintenance, Ken Cassens, has already built the steel tube framework fuselage and undercarriage over the last two winters. Using some original Ryan Brougham parts, Ken is striving to make this repro the closest in detail in every respect to that of the original, which is on display at the Air and Space Museum, Washington DC. Ken has visited the original *Spirit* and made detailed measurements of the aircraft from a 'cherry picker' to verify his plans and measurements. Someone at Old Rhinebeck remarked, 'It will be a shame to cover the fuselage as the welding job is a work of art in itself.' The aircraft will be fitted with period flight instruments and will have an original Wright Whirlwind engine up front, just like the original's. Its first flight is scheduled for 1999 or 2000.

In July 1997 it was the turn of the Caudron G.III replica to have its first major check, rebuild and re-cover since it was built in 1986. ORA mechanic Tim Moore was working on this project, and despite the fact that it looked more like a twelve-month job, he was hoping to get it reassembled and re-covered inside two months in time for a commemorative airshow. Old Rhinebeck's Caudron was powered by an 80 hp Le Rhône rotary before the strip-down, but as this engine has been switched to the Nieuport 11 and the Nieuport's engine is in the workshop for maintenance, they will be swopped. This rotary engine switching is a fairly normal flying museum

phenomenon these days as they have only a limited number of serviceable engines to go around.

Old Rhinebeck's Curtiss Fledgling, which is a civilianized version of the US Navy N2c-1 trainer dating from the late 1920s, has served them well over the years. It has flown in almost every act they have tried. It has now been decided that this lovely big old biplane should be restored to flying condition again after a lay-off of a couple of years. I found that their plan for disassembling the aircraft was quite simple – wait for an airshow morning when there will be lots of helpers available to get the (nearly twenty feet either side) wings off. This will start as a winter project for the ORA restoration teams. The fuselage will be roaded to Gene DeMarco's facility in Florida, the wings will be farmed out somewhere else and the 220 hp Continental will be worked on by yet another specialist. When restoration of these individual components is complete they will be brought back to Old Rhinebeck for final assembly and test flying.

Up in the Pioneer Hangar Andy Ross is rebuilding a Wright brothers Glider based on their 1902 experiments. Apart from working on this project in the hangar, Andy also encourages the public to ask questions about these early aeroplanes. He also gets to show them his woodcraft abilities, and the early rigging techniques which have been all but forgotten by the majority of people over the passage of time.

The three old museum hangars at the top of the hill are starting to let in the elements, not to mention the wildlife, birds and insects. While I was there a couple of chipmunks were having a great time chasing each other inside the hangar roof. The other problem in the winter is the possibility of heavy snowfall causing a roof collapse. Cole would have agreed that the three original museum hangars are more like holding hangars for injured and bruised machines than a proper museum facility. These priceless aircraft should be kept dry and safe, then there is always the possibility that they may be made to fly again. These hangars, and those housing the 'flyers' on the aerodrome, will be improved over the next few years as money from special fund-raising events starts to become available. One thing is for sure though, none of the atmosphere of these buildings will be lost because the self-governing criterion for the trustees will be – 'Would Cole have approved?' This philosophy is also the determining

The Sopwith Dolphin on a test flight with Cole Palen in September 1990. Two weeks later it was to suffer an in-flight engine failure.

factor on how future restorations and rebuilds are handled. Cole was very quick at making decisions about rebuilds and restoration projects, and sticking to them. Jim Hare reflected on the nature of future plans:

The airshows are more or less self-financing but our membership is vital to the survival of Rhinebeck Aerodrome Museum. We get generous donations from time to time and we are currently getting corporate support and sponsorship from local businesses. We are also looking for special grants in the near future. In the past most of the money was invested in the aircraft but now that we have around sixty aircraft we need to protect and preserve them properly in better buildings. There will always be airworthy rotary-powered aircraft at Old Rhinebeck. But to conserve our valuable rotaries we will consider adding more reliable radials to our collection. By doing this we can take part in airshows farther afield by taking airplanes, particularly our World War One machines, to them either by road or air. This will give us a far higher profile away from home so that potential visitors will want to visit Old Rhinebeck to see the whole show.

To illustrate his point he instanced Brian Coughlin's Fokker D.VIII reproduction, which is based at Old Rhinebeck. 'It's got a 160 hp Gnôme rotary and the first engine that Brian fitted only lasted for nine hours' flying time before needing an overhaul; finding and replacing these engines is difficult and expensive. Rotary engine time has to be conserved. This is the same problem faced by all flying museums around the world still flying rotaries. The engines are now getting very old and very scarce.

Promoting the aerodrome is necessary in order to raise the funding needed to restore and preserve these magnificent machines; 1997 saw two away trips for Old Rhinebeck's aeroplanes. In April the first significant 'road trip' in over thirty years was made to Sun 'N' Fun at Lakeland, Florida where the Nieuport 11 'Bébé' and the Fokker Dr.1 were displayed. Sun 'N' Fun's experts reckoned that it was the first time a rotary-powered aircraft had graced their skies. After this both aircraft were taken apart again and trailered to MacDill AFB south of Tampa, where with their wings back on they were loaded on board a C-5A Galaxy and flown to the 'Golden Air Tattoo' airshow at Nellis AFB for the USAF's fiftieth anniversary celebrations. Here a crowd of around

500,000 people found out that Cole Palen's 'Air Force' was still alive and well. 'This spirit of going out to the people is very much what Cole did in the early days and we hope it will pay dividends as our profile is raised with the public,' commented Jim Hare.

ORA's superb repro Albatros D.Va, built by Cole Palen, was at the time of writing waiting to have a new crankshaft fitted to its 175 hp Ranger engine. It was being stored in the Lindbergh Era hangar. Leading German fighter ace Baron Manfred von Richthofen, better known as the 'Red Baron', and more famous for his Fokker Dr.1 exploits, in fact accounted for more 'kills' while flying an Albatros D.Va than in his all-red Fokker Triplanes.

ABOVE:
Another New Standard D-25 fuselage complete with engine awaits the call of the restorers in the 'Dawn Patrol' aerodrome hangar.

BELOW:
Yet another New Standard D-25 fuselage, complete with engine patiently awaits rescue.

Brian Coughlin is trying to prise the bottom wing away from the fuselage of the Curtiss Fledgling so that the aircraft can be resurrected. He is watched by one of his fans, who is definitely an aspiring pilot and restorer in the making.

Bill King checks out the top wing of the Fledgling. 'Get ready, there's not much holding it now,' he says.

Off at last! Both wings come off in one piece so that they can be easily disassembled on the ground.

ABOVE:
Some of the Caudron G.III's wing ribs have been cleaned up and checked ready for reassembly.

RIGHT:
Tim Moore, a mechanic at ORA, has his hands full amongst the innards of the Caudron G.III. It was a thrill just watching him take out parts, clean them, then neatly lay them out ready for re-assembly. With ten years of oil and gunge sticking to the aeroplane it is difficult to appreciate that this is a repro and not an original aircraft.

From the side, the pilot's seat of the Caudron can be seen just above Tim's head. This part of the aircraft looks relatively small, but with the engine to be added and two huge wings to be erected this is no small project to be turned around within a couple of months.

During the week the museum buildings are a peaceful oasis. Period music drifts gently from the hangars and you are free to roam amongst this wonderful collection for as long as you like. Sit on a bench and soak up the atmosphere or enjoy a leisurely picnic; wander down the hill through the parking lot to the airfield and glance into the Fokker and A.V. Roe hangars or the 'Royal Aircraft Factory' to see the planes that will fly during the weekend shows – pioneer planes chronicle the history of flight on Saturdays, and Sundays feature World War One and barnstorming aircraft. Plan to come back and see these remarkable planes take to the skies. If you happen to come on a show day you will still find the museum open, except during showtime.

The following descriptions show the aircraft on display in each of the four museum hangars in July 1997

In the new **Museum Building** all the airplanes are original except for the unfinished reproduction of the *Spirit of St Louis*. A stroll along the walkways will bring all sorts of fascinating aeroplanes and memorabilia to light.

The original **Voisin** takes pride of place and by its sheer size dominates the hangar. Designed by Gabriel and Charles Voisin of France, the museum's example was built in 1909 by Norvin C. Rinek who incorporated many ideas of his own in the construction. Although outwardly this machine appears very similar to the Voisin-produced aircraft it differs in many ways. Most notably Rinek became the first to utilize a chrome-moly welded steel tube structure in place of the standard wooden frame. This machine is believed to have

An original Voisin at the entrance to the new Museum Building (on your right at the top of the hill) was nosed out of the building especially for this book. All aircraft within are originals, except for the Spirit of St Louis.

flown up to six times before being stored in the roof of Rinek's rope factory for over sixty years. Despite the type's marginal controllability it set many records and is largely responsible for creating interest in aviation amongst all Europeans. Henri Farman accomplished the first circular and kilometre flight in Europe in one and it was these publicized flights that brought the Voisins to the notice of Norvin Rinek of Easton, Pennsylvania. Cole Palen acquired and restored the airplane in 1973.

A **Blériot XI** manufactured by the American Aeroplane Supply House of Hempstead, New York has a 70 hp Gnôme engine and is an example of the cross-country Blériot which won all major European air races in 1911. In the USA it made the first demonstration air mail flight by Earle Ovington.

The **Fleet 16B**, a popular training and sport aircraft, was built uninterrupted from 1929 through to 1945. The museum's example, with its 125 hp Kinner engine, was built in Canada in 1942 and was used as a basic trainer for the RCAF. It flew at Old Rhinebeck from 1966 to 1986.

The **Fairchild F-24-H** was bought as a $10,000 Christmas present by a New York stockbroker for his wife. The machine was impressed into military service as a UC-61 during World War Two and flew sub-patrols carrying two one-hundred-pound bombs. One submarine sinking was claimed.

The 1929 **New Standard D-25** was manufactured by the New Standard Aircraft Corp., Paterson, New Jersey and was designed by Charles Healy Day. It would have been fitted originally with a 220 hp Wright Whirlwind nine-cylinder radial for its barnstorming activities. This machine is fitted with a 220 hp Continental radial engine; it carried four fare-paying passengers, was easy to fly and operated out of the smallest fields. This was the aerodrome's first New Standard and carried over 11,000 passengers on weekend rides during its career.

The Fleet 16B in the new Museum Building.

The **American Eagle A-129** was a popular biplane dating from 1929, with a top speed of 105 mph from its 100 hp Kinner K5 air-cooled five-cylinder radial engine. Manufactured by the American Eagle Aircraft Corp. of Kansas City it seats a pilot and two passengers. It was originally designed for a war-surplus Curtiss OX-5 engine which was available at low cost, but when the lighter, air-cooled engines like the Kinner became available, the nose of the plane had to be lengthened to maintain aerodynamic balance. This was quite obvious on the American Eagle and the Kinner-powered version became known as the 'ant-eater'. The American Eagle was safe and easy to fly and was used by many flying schools. This airplane was donated by Paul Richards (now an ORA trustee) who was known for flying down the Hudson River at low level alongside passenger trains, matching their speed while delighted train passengers waved and snapped pictures.

The museum's **Morane Saulnier A-1** was purchased along with another A-1 by Cole Palen at an auction in 1978 and was restored in 1980. It flew at ORA for several years. The second A-1 was converted to a Morane Saulnier N during restoration and is on display in the World War One building. The type dates from 1917 when Robert and Leon Morane and Raymond Saulnier presented this, their latest fighter aircraft, to the French military for review. It was accepted and produced in large numbers. Despite the fact that the Morane's flight characteristics were well liked by many pilots its active service was limited to three months. It was withdrawn from combat as a result of alleged structural failures and reliability problems with the 160 hp Gnôme engine. Many remaining aircraft were refitted with smaller, more reliable power plants and used as advanced trainers for the duration of the war and afterwards.

A **Ryan NYP *Spirit of St Louis*** reproduction is currently being built to exacting standards by Ken Cassens, ORA's director of maintenance.

A close-up from the rear of the Voisin's beautifully restored V-8 Rinek engine, also note the vertical radiator mounted behind the pilot's seat.

BLÉRIOT XI
FRENCH DESIGN-1911
MFG. AMERICAN AEROPLANE SUPPLY HOUSE
HEMSTEAD, N.Y.
ENGINE - 70 HP GNOME

THIS ORIGINAL AIRCRAFT IS AN
EXAMPLE OF THE CROSS-COUNTRY
BLERIOT WHICH WON ALL MAJOR
EUROPEAN AIR RACES IN 1911:
PARIS TO ROME, CIRCUIT OF
BRITAIN, CIRCUIT OF EUROPE.
USING NAVAL NAVIGATION METHODS,
ANDRE BEAUMONT WON MOST OF THESE
RACES USING A WATCH, COMPASS
AND A MAP ON ROLLERS.
IN THIS COUNTRY IT MADE THE
1ST DEMONSTRATION AIR MAIL
... GARDEN CITY TO MINEOLA, ... OVINGTON.

A Blériot XI machine, powered by a 70 hp Gnôme rotary, in the new Museum Building.

ABOVE:
The gutsy 160 hp Gnôme rotary-powered Morane A.1 before semi-retirement to the museum.

BELOW:
An original Morane A.1 from World War One and right is the reproduction Spirit of St Louis *being built to flying condition by Ken Cassens. Behind is the tail assembly of the Voisin.*

An American Eagle A-129, N513H, s/n 534, in the new Museum Building.

In the **Pioneer Hangar** are the earliest flying machines on show at the museum.

A **Wright Glider** from 1902 is under restoration. This is a reproduction of the first heavier-than-air machine that had a mechanical control system. It was the basis for the Wright brothers' patent application filed in 1903.

The **Short S-29** replica dates from 1909 and has an original ENV (1909–10) engine fitted which gave it a typical flying speed for the era of 35 to 40 mph. This is one of the many Farman type copies of the period. The engine in this aircraft was flown by Cecil Grace in an S-27 at the Bournemouth, England air meet in 1910; it was later removed from an S-29 prior to his attempt for the Baron De Forest prize.

The French **Deperdussin** is a copy of an outstanding historical aircraft of unusually modern lines, first designed in 1912 and the winner of the famous Gordon Bennett Trophy two years in a row. The structure and streamlining were made possible by the advanced use of the very strong monocoque plywood structure which made it the first airplane to exceed 100 mph. The designer, Bechereau, was retained by Louis Blériot when he took over the Deperdussin firm, and eventually this combination built the famous SPAD fighters of World War One.

A Blériot XI from 1910 has a 25 hp Anzani three-cylinder air-cooled radial engine and a top speed of about 42 mph. This type was Louis Blériot's eleventh design and his first really successful airplane. After witnessing a flight by Wilbur Wright in 1908 he abandoned his pivoting wing tips and copied the Wright system of warping or twisting the wings for lateral (banking) control. On 25 July 1909 Blériot was the first to fly across the English Channel in a machine very similar to this. Halfway across he lost sight of land and, lacking a compass, arrived off course. When he landed a Customs officer arrived on the scene and recorded Blériot's craft as a yacht named *Aeroplane*.

In the roof hangs a **Thomas Pusher model 2**, an American airplane from 1912 with a 90 hp Curtiss OX –5 engine. This aircraft is one of twelve manufactured by W.T. Thomas, Bath, New York. It was his second design and in November 1912 an aircraft of this type established the two-place world endurance record, flying for three hours fifty-two minutes. This aircraft was flown from ORA to New York city where it and its pilot Cole Palen appeared on the TV program *I've Got A Secret*.

A 1911 **Nieuport 2N** reproduction built by Cole is being restored. It was obviously very tail heavy so we'll have to wait to see if it flies this time.

OPPOSITE:
Overhead is a 1912 Thomas Pusher reproduction, while beneath is a Short S-29 repro, and to the right is a Deperdussin monocoque racer repro. You will find these in the Pioneer hangar.

Visitors to the Pioneer hangar can often meet Andy Ross – today he is working on the Wright Glider.

The Pioneer hangar is situated at the top of the hill and is the left
one of the three hangars. Inside on the left are early Wright brothers
reproduction gliders and on the right can be seen a Nieuport 2N
repro, made by Cole, which is about to be re-covered again.

ABOVE:
This Curtiss-Wright CW-1 Junior is kept dry in the roof of the 'Dawn Patrol' hangar on the aerodrome. This very early minimum aeroplane was regularly flown by Cole.

BELOW:
The French-designed Caudron G.III appeared in war paint during 1914 and was used by them and the British 'Royal Flying Corps' in the reconnaissance role. Over 1,400 of the type were produced by the home-based Caudron Company alone, while smaller batches were produced in England by the British Caudron Company. They were powered by rotary and radial engines from the period; the 80 hp Gnôme was the preferred rotary while 80 hp and 100 hp Anzani radials were equally successful.

The World War One hangar is situated in the center of the three hangars at the top of the hill. The engineless Morane Saulnier Type 'N' dominates overhead, while on the left is the Sopwith Dolphin, and right the Davis D-1W (stored there awaiting restoration, as is the Albatros D.Va from World War One).

The **World War One Hangar** contains many famous names. Take a trip down the gangway for a nostalgic step back in time.

An authentic reproduction **Sopwith Dolphin** was built by Andy Keefe and Cole Palen in 1977 from Hawker-Siddeley drawings. It is equipped with an original 180 hp Hispano-Suiza engine. The Dolphin was at first received into British squadrons with skepticism. The pilot, flying the first multi-gun fighter in history, sat head level with the center section enabling him to look over or under the top wing. He sat with the engine practically in his lap, twin fixed Vickers machine-guns mounted above the engine, and twin Lewis machine-guns mounted on the top wing (early models) were inches from his face. The gas tank was behind his head. The craft was also capable of carrying four 25 lb Cooper bombs. Dolphins proved themselves flying top cover at the 18 to 20,000 ft level. There were 1,532 built. This craft flew at ORA from 1977 until 30 September 1990 when it made an unscheduled landing in trees due to engine failure. Pilot Dick King was uninjured. The aircraft is being rebuilt and should be flying again in 1999. There are no known original **Fokker Dr.1 Triplanes** in existence. The museum's copy was constructed in 1967 by Cole Palen. It is complete with a 110 hp Le Rhône rotary engine and was designed using drawings from several sources, including those made by the British in 1918 from a captured aircraft. This aircraft played a major role in the growth of Old Rhinebeck, dogfighting Dick King's authentic Sopwith Pup reproduction for many years. After twenty years of continual use, flying in nearly every Sunday show, it was retired. The original Fokker Dr.1s, or Triplanes as they are popularly known, combined excellent maneuverability with a high rate of climb. The type was favored by Manfred von Richthofen and Werner Voss, two of Germany's legendary fighter pilots. Both lost their lives in this type.

Fokker Dr.1 Triplane reproduction registered N3221, s/n 322, built by Cole Palen, features in the World War One hangar.

The museum's **Nieuport model 10** is an original aircraft which is said to have been brought to the US in 1924 by the famous French ace Charles Nungesser. He took the aircraft to Roosevelt Field on Long Island to film the First World War movie *The Sky Raider*. In 1951 the National Air and Space Museum acquired the aircraft and in 1986 traded it for Cole Palen's original Nieuport 28. Cole restored the Nieuport 10 and painted the black heart with skull and crossbones (Charles Nungesser's personal wartime insignia) on the sides. It flew at ORA from 1987 to 1990. The type originates from 1915 and was the first in the long and successful series of Nieuport 'V' strutters. It was used primarily for observation, however; many were converted to single-seat fighters by simply covering the front cockpit, and adding an upward-firing Lewis machine-gun to the center section of the top wing. When the Nieuport 11 (factory-produced single-seat fighter) appeared at the Front, the main duty of the model 10 became that of a training machine. There were several variants of this basic design which were used not only by the French, but also by the Americans and Russians.

In 1992 construction of this reproduction Italian **Ansaldo A-1 'Balilla'** from 1917 was started by Andy Keefe after an original 160 hp Isotta-Fraschini engine was procured from the Caproni Collection in Italy. It was one of the fastest aircraft to be designed during the First World War, achieving a speed of nearly 140 mph. In addition to its great speed, the type was noted for its exceptional rate of climb. The pilot was also allowed an excellent field of view due to the 'V'-shaped design of the plywood fuselage. Despite being nearly 30 mph faster than any other fighter of the time it was not well received by the top Italian pilots. It was said to lack maneuverability and was never considered suitable for service at the Front. It was produced in limited quantities and was used primarily as a home defence fighter. Poland purchased thirty-four of these aircraft, with a license from Ansaldo to produce an additional sixty aircraft for its air force between 1920 and 1924.

Overhead Cole's 1959 pink Cadillac, which is parked at the end of this hangar, you will see a **Pigeon-Fraser Albree Scout**, an American craft from 1917. It was the first pursuit aircraft contracted for by the United States, but only three were built. The first was static-tested to destruction and the second crashed and burned on its maiden flight, killing the test pilot. One scorched wing panel was repaired and installed in this, the unfinished third aircraft. Then the US government canceled the contract, so this last remaining aircraft was stored in the rafters of the Pigeon Hollow Spar Co. in Boston, Massachusetts for forty-four years. Then on 15 November 1961 Cole Palen procured it for ORA. It is a prize example of an unsuccessful aircraft.

A reproduction **Siemens-Schuckert D.111** built by Cole in 1969 has a 160 hp Gnôme as no Siemens Halske (the original engine for the type) was available at the time of construction. It has been taxied but never flown. The original had a maximum speed of 112 mph, a climb rate of six minutes to

9,500 feet and an endurance of two hours. It was best known for its phenomenal rate of climb, but in addition to overheating problems it demanded an excellent pilot, particularly on landings. Many front-line pilots found themselves hanging upside down by their shoulder harness seconds after touchdown.

A very rare **Thomas Morse S-4B** was discovered in a barn in Wisconsin during 1954. It was restored by Dwight Woodward and flown at the Aerodrome for several years. It is an American craft of 1917–18 vintage with a 80 hp Le Rhône engine. It was the result of an American effort to produce a fighter type for the Great War, but was never used for this purpose and became an advanced pursuit trainer. This example is the last of the 100 S-4Bs built.

A picture of a **Nieuport 2N** was all the inspiration Cole needed to build this reproduction. The original would have dated from 1911. It is being restored to appear in the pioneer aircraft Saturday shows but has never flown as it was found to be tail heavy – let's hope for better things next time the engine starts running.

'Flying' overhead at the front of this hangar is a **Morane Saulnier 'N',** considered by many to be the grand-daddy of the modern fighter plane. A French craft dating from 1914 it has a 80 hp Le Rhône engine. The 'N' was the first to carry a forward-firing machine-gun and triangular steel plates on the back of the propeller blade deflected the bullets. Ivan Smirnov of the Imperial Russian Army used a boat anchor on a rope trailing behind his Morane to pull the wings off enemy aircraft.

OPPOSITE:
Cole's 1959 pink Cadillac, still with the ignition keys in, has the only surviving Pigeon-Fraser Albree Scout hanging inverted above it in the World War One hangar.

ORA volunteer Hugo Visconti gives a guided tour of the museum hangars to a group of visitors. They are pictured in the World War One hangar; the aircraft overhead is a Morane Saulnier Type 'N'.

Siemens-Schuckert D-111 reproduction, N1918G, was built by Cole and is housed in the World War One hangar.

ABOVE:
Thomas Morse S-4B, N74W, s/n 153, pictured in the World War One hangar.

BELOW:
This original Nieuport 10 can be found in the World War One hangar.

The Ansaldo A-1 Balilla reproduction can be seen in the confines of the World War One hangar.

Known as the Lindbergh Era hangar, it is the farthest to the right of the three hangars at the top of the hill. Inside the hangar on the left is a Pitcairn Mailwing, on the right is a Monocoupe 90, and overhead a Monocoupe 113.

The **Lindbergh Era** is celebrated with a hangar full of magnificent machines from this period.

A **Pitcairn Mailwing** from 1929 has a 220 hp Continental engine. It was designed to carry the early night air mail as it had excellent maneuverability, range and speed (130 mph) and at the time was considered the very modern equivalent of the Pony Express. In later years, because of their excellent load carrying ability, Pitcairns became popular as crop dusters. This plane was flown from Vancouver to Old Rhinebeck aerodrome in thirty-three hours. It flew at Old Rhinebeck from 1963 to 1980.

The **Morane Saulnier MS.130** dates from 1927 and is fitted with a Salmson 230 hp engine. One of the oldest and most famous names in French aviation history, their first aircraft appeared in 1911 and the name still lives on today. Morane Saulnier MS.130s became favorites with French aerobatics pilots, but it was originally designed as an advanced trainer, light reconnaissance and postal aircraft. Some 143 were ordered by the French Navy and they are still sought after by pilots and collectors alike.

The '**Waco' Model 10** was manufactured by the Advance Aircraft Co. of Troy, Ohio and is an example of a classic American aircraft remembered for its training role and sport flying. It was also used as a 'mail plane' by some of the early airlines. This model was so popular that 350 of the 90 hp Curtiss OX-5 versions were produced in 1927 alone. They had a maximum speed of 97 mph, a cruise of 84 mph, landed at 37 mph, had a ceiling of 12,000 feet and a range of 385 miles. This aeroplane crashed in about 1930 and was rebuilt at Naples, New York. During its career it once landed in a tree and another time finished up inverted.

The **Spartan C-3-165** dates from 1929 and is a very good example of the average general aircraft developed to that date. Fitted with a 165 hp Wright J6 radial engine this model had a cruising speed of 100 mph. It was rugged, dependable and performed a wide variety of services. It was manufactured by the Spartan Aircraft Co, Tulsa, Oklahoma, and had a price tag of $6,750 in 1929.

The **Pietenpol Air Camper** from 1933 was designed in the late 1920s for the Depression-stricken airmen. It was a popular home-built that could be made inexpensively. Designed to get good performance out of a 40 hp Model A Ford engine, it fulfilled all of Bernie Pietenpol's visions with the exception of its poor climb rate. This aircraft, which is currently on skis, was built by Karl Erickson (one of ORA's pioneer aircraft pilots) as he enjoys flying off snow.

Overhead, a **Heath Parasol LNA-40** which originated from American airplane designer Edward Heath in 1932. He marketed plans for his diminutive home-built aircraft which was powered by a converted motorcycle engine in 1927. By 1932 Heath won its approved type certificate and it became available with the new Continental A-40. It could be built from plans or factory-assembled parts, or purchased complete from the factory. Three wing variations could be used; the museum's example is the clipped wing type for sport racing.

This **Aeromarine-Klemm AKL-26** dates from 1929 and is powered by a 65 hp Le Blonde five-cylinder radial. Built at Keyport, New Jersey, the type was built under license from the German Klemm company and was very successful. They were built in many countries around the world and were known for their easy handling and slow flight characteristics. The aircraft is of all wood construction built to be disassembled in minutes, towed behind a car and stored in a garage.

The museum's **Bird Model CK** dates from 1931 and was barnstormed at Old Rhinebeck for many years. It is capable of carrying three passengers in the front cockpit or 540 lb of cargo. They were produced by the Bird Aircraft Corp. of Glendale, Long Island, New York, but only forty-two of these Kinner B-5, 125 hp powered machines were manufactured.

Hanging from the roof of this hangar is a replica of a **Dickson Primary Glider** which was made from original 1930 drawings. This glider is typical of many gliders of the Lindbergh era. It was a low-cost way to get into the air and could be launched either by stretched rubber cord or auto tow, and was easily assembled or disassembled in minutes.

The **Nicholas-Beazley NB-8G** monoplane has an unusual feature: its wings fold back to a width of just over ten feet for easier storage; however there were a few examples of the wing locking device not being reliable and causing mid-air accidents. As a light two-seat sport trainer its gentle nature made it a favorite with instructors of the day and it was quickly recommended by all who flew in it. At least fifty-seven of these not pretty, open-cockpit 'parasol' monoplanes were built. With its 80 hp Armstrong-Siddeley 'Genet' cowled engine the aircraft had sufficient muscle to deliver a commendable performance for 'sportsmen' too.

A **Link Trainer** dating from 1935–45 is also here as a reminder to all of the importance of 'blind flying' or flying on instruments. This electrically powered device could simulate all altitudes and conditions of flight, and the duplicated instrument readings and the course plotted could be checked by the instructor at his desk.

The Mono Aircraft Co. **Monocoupe 90**, powered by a 90 hp Lambert, was a speedy 120 mph sport aircraft which stayed in production throughout the Depression and was further developed into an even more successful machine. Over 1,000 Monocoupes were built up to 1934. Monocoupes were flown in cross-country and pylon races by Phoebe Omlie, Johnny Livingston and Vern Roberts, and in 1930 Phoebe Omlie's winnings totaled $3,250 when the national hourly wage was half a cent.

Overhead, a **Monocoupe 113** from 1929 is fitted with a 60 hp Velie engine. Clayton Folkerts built the original 1927 Monocoupe to the requirements of Don Luscombe and it was the first cabin two-seater to achieve popularity in the US. For years it was a favorite with racing pilots. Some 350 Velie coupes were built.

Individual aero-engines in this hangar include the Cirrus 90 upright air-cooled, the Curtiss C-6, the Gipsy 90 hp upright air-cooled, the Heath Henderson (1925), the Salmson 40 hp (1926), the Siemens-Halske, the Szekely 30 hp (1928), the Szekely 45 hp (1930), the Liberty V12, the Renault V12, the 120 hp Mercedes, and the Curtiss OX-5.

Overhead at the back of the Lindbergh Era hangar is this Heath Parasol LNA-40, and under it can be seen a Dickson Primary Glider, N5666, built by Cole Palen.

'Waco' Model 10, N940, s/n 751 is another classic American light aircraft survivor on view in the Lindbergh Era hangar.

OPPOSITE TOP:
Monocoupe 90, N429N, in the Lindbergh Era hangar.

OPPOSITE BOTTOM:
Bird Model CK, N850W – Lindbergh Era hangar.

BELOW:
Pitcairn Mailwing, N15307 – Lindbergh Era hangar.

PITCAIRN MAILWING
AMERICAN 1929
ENGINE: 220 H.P. CONTINENTAL
DESIGNED TO CARRY THE NIGHT
AIR MAIL. IT HAD EXCELLENT
MANEUVERABILITY, RANGE, SPEED
(130 MPH) AND WAS CONSIDERED
A VERY MODERN EQUIVALENT OF
THE PONY EXPRESS IN 1929.
IN LATER YEARS, BECAUSE OF
ITS LOAD-CARRYING ABILITY,
PITCAIRNS BECAME POPULAR AS
DUSTERS.
RECENTLY REBUILT, THIS PLANE
WAS FLOWN FROM VANCOUVER, WASH.
TO THE AERODROME IN 33 HRS.
FLYING AT O.R.A. 1963-1980

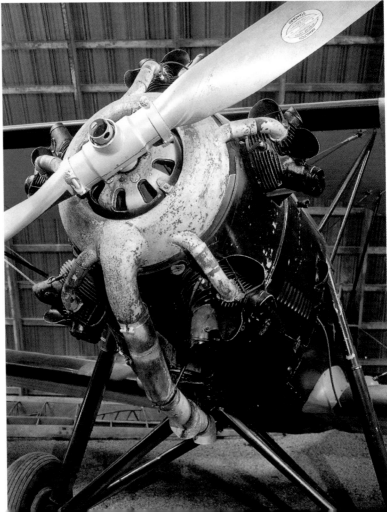

ABOVE:
Spartan C-3-165, NC285M can be found in the Lindbergh Era hangar.

RIGHT:
Close-up of Spartan C-3-165's 165 hp Wright J6 five-cylinder radial.

Out for an airing, this Nicholas-Beazley NB-8G lives in the Lindbergh Era hangar.

Named Spirit of Old Rhinebeck, *this Monocoupe 113, N8955,
greets you from overhead as you enter the Lindbergh Era hangar.*

To utilize maximum space at Old Rhinebeck quite a few of the aircraft are parked like this Piper Cub, pictured in the 'Dawn Patrol' aerodrome hangar.

Gene DeMarco opens up this off-limits treasure trove. Old Rhinebeck's storage area might look a bit of a shambles but Gene knew every part that was there – spare wings, engines, the lot. The fuselage by Gene's knee is another New Standard D-25 making five of these airframes available to the museum. Above him is a Fokker E.III Eindekker fuselage reproduction; to the right of this is a fuselage of a repro Ryan NYP which will probably be finished to static condition so that the public can try it out for size. To the right of that is an original Kreider-Reisner KR-31 complete with Curtiss OX-5 engine.

Still in the storage area, Gene has his hand resting on ORA's 1927 Kreider-Reisner KR-31 biplane. Amos H. Kreider and L.E. Reisner had been associated earlier with the 'Waco' and set up their own company at Hagerstown, Maryland to produce their own three-place biplane. Nine aircraft of this model number were produced in 1927 with narrow vertically mounted radiators between the engine and the top wing – something else for the long-suffering 1920s pilot to get his head around. Let's hope that this machine will eventually be restored to flying condition!

John Barker, who was the Black Baron for many years, taxies his
Tavelair 4000 Speedwing down to the pumps. John rebuilt this
beautiful machine from the remains of a Travelair 4000 which had
been converted to a crop sprayer. He and wife Pam, who has rebuilt
her own WACO RNF, roaded John's aircraft all the way from Oregon
to New York State.

She's big but she never was particularly beautiful: ORA's Curtiss Fledgling pictured a few years before she was laid up for complete restoration in 1997. She might even be flying again before this book hits the shelves.

OLD RHINEBECK AIRCRAFT (JULY 1997)

Name	N number	Serial No.	Manufacturer	Status
Aeromarine 39B	-	-	Aeromarine	S
Aeronca C-3	N17447	A754	Aeronautical Corp. of America	F
Aeromarine-Klemm AKL-26	N320N	2-59	Aeromarine-Klemm Corp.	M
Albatros D-Va	N12156	17-D-7517	Palen	M/R
American Eagle A-129	N513H	534	American Eagle Aircraft Corp.	M
Ansaldo A-1 'Balilla'	-	-	Keefe	M
Avro 504K	N4929	HAC1	Hampshire Avro	F
Balloon – Picard AX3M	N7132	23	Picard	M
Bird Model CK	N850W	4012	Bird Aircraft Corp.	M
Blériot XI	N60094	56	Blériot	F
Blériot XI	N99923	3856	American Aeroplane Supply House	M
Blériot XI	-	153	Palen/Blériot	M
Caudron G-3	N3943P	1914–2	Palen	R
Curtiss Fledgling	N271Y	8–52	Curtiss-Wright Airplane Co.	R
Curtiss Jenny JN-4H	N3918	3919	Curtiss-Wright Airplane Co.	F
Curtiss Pusher	N4124A	2	Palen	L
Curtiss 'D' Pusher	N68014	1976	Palen	F
Curtiss-Wright Junior	N605EB	1025	Curtiss-Wright Airplane Co.	F
Davis D-1-W	N532K	115	Davis Aircraft Co.	M/R
Demoiselle H-2	N6551	1	Gazelle	F
Demoiselle	-	-	Taylor/Palen	R
Deperdussin	N8448	11	Palen	M
Dickson Primary Glider	N5666	PHC-1	Palen	M
Fairchild F-24-H	-	-	Fairchild Aircraft Co.	M
F.E.8	N17501	300	Palen	L
Fokker E.III	-	-	Old Rhinebeck Aerodrome Museum	S
Fokker Dr.I	N3221	322	Palen	M
Fokker Dr.I	N209R	425	William Winter	L
Fokker F.1. Triplane	N220TP	F1-103	Palmer-Wilgus	F
Fokker D.VII	N70814	1918–1989	Palen	F
Fokker D.VIII	N94100	941	Coughlin	P/O/F
Fleet Finch 16B	N666J	350	Fleet Aircraft Inc.	M
Great Lakes 2-T-1MS	N304Y	191	Great Lakes Aircraft Corp.	F
Hanriot	N8449	11	Palen	F
Heath Parasol LNA-40	N5719	1000	Heath Aircraft Corp.	M
Kreider-Reisner KR-31	-	-	Kreider-Reisner Aircraft Co.	S
Monocoupe 90	N429N	618	Mono Aircraft Corp.	M
Monocoupe 113	N8955	322	Mono Aircraft Corp.	M
Morane Saulnier MS.130	N7MS	001	Morane Saulnier	M
Morane Saulnier A1	N1379M	417	Morane Saulnier	M
Morane Saulnier 'N'	N5356J	1915–84	Palen	M
Nieuport 2 N	N9147A	1911–78	Palen	M
Nieuport 10	N680CP	680	Nieuport	M
Nieuport 11	N9163A	1915–78	Palen	F
New Standard D-25	N19155	160J	New Standard Aircraft Corp.	F
New Standard D-25	N176H	138	White	M
Nicholas-Beazley NB-8G	N576Y	K-18	Nicholas-Beazley Airplane Div.	M
Pietenpol Air Camper	NX6262	-	Erickson	P/O/M
Pigeon-Fraser Albree Scout	-	-	Pigeon Hollow Spar Co.	M
Pitcairn Mailwing	N15307	-	Pitcairn Aircraft	M
Puss Moth	N770N	2140	de Havilland	S
Raab-Katzenstein Glider	-	-	-	M
Ryan NYP	-	-	Old Rhinebeck Aerodrome Museum	U/C/M
Siemens-Schuckert D-III	N1918G	1918–70	Palen	M
Short S-29	N4275	2	Palen	M

Name	Number	Serial No.	Manufacturer	Status
Sopwith Camel	N7157Q	1990	Palen	F
Sopwith Dolphin	N47166	1533	Palen/Keefe	M/R
Spartan C-3	N285M	120	Spartan Aircraft Co.	M
Stampe SV-4B	N255V	-	Société Stampe et Vertongen	P/O/F
Stearman PT-17	N61116	-	Boeing Aircraft Co.	P/O/F
Taylor Cub J-2	N17834	1269	Taylor Aircraft	F
Thomas Morse S-4B	N74W	153	Thomas-Morse Aircraft Corp	M
Thomas Pusher Model 2	N4720G	2	W.T. Thomas	M
Tiger Moth	G-ACDC	-	de Havilland	P/O/F
Voisin	N38933	1	Norvin C. Renik	M
'Waco' Model 9	-	-	Advance Aircraft Co.	L
'Waco' Model 10	N940	751	Advance Aircraft Co.	M
Wright Brothers Glider	-	-	Palen	M/R
Wright 'Vin Fiz'	N1911P	1911–1981	Palen	S

Key to status symbols

F – flying **M** – museum

P/O – privately owned **R** – restoration

U/C – new subject under construction **L** – away from the Collection on loan

S – stored, probably in parts and generally not on show to the public

This Davis D-1W, dating from 1929, would have been fitted originally with a 110 hp Warner radial, hence the 'W' designation. It is in fact now powered by a 125 hp Warner power-plant. This classic sport aeroplane was conceived by the Vulcan Aircraft Company as the American answer to the success of de Havilland's Moth series of biplanes in England. They came to greater prominence when ex-auto maker Walter Davis acquired the manufacturing rights, but due to the economic climate of the time only about sixty of these beautiful parasol-winged monoplanes were built.

*The Black Baron of Rhinebeck comes home in his Triplane after a
day's work at the Sunday show!*